Door to the Diamond Way

by
Je Tsongkapa
(1357–1419)

with a commentary by
Pabongka Rinpoche
Dechen Nyingpo
(1878–1941)

translated by
Khen Rinpoche
Geshe Lobsang Tharchin
with
Geshe Michael Roach

Published by
The Diamond Cutter Press
6490 State Route 179
Sedona, Arizona 86351-7978
United States

Library of Congress Cataloging in Publication Data [*sic:*]

Tsoṅ-kha-pa Blo-bzaṅ-grags-pa, 1357–1419
Preparing for Tantra
The Mountain of Blessings
(Classics of Middle Asia)
Translation of: Yon-tan-gzhir-gyur-ma'i-grel-pa.
Bibliography: p.
l. Tsoṅ-kha-pa Blo-bzaṅ-grags-pa, 1357–1419.
Yon-tan-gzhir-gyur-ma'i-grel-pa. 2. Buddhism—Doctrines.
3. Dge-lugs-pa (Sect)—Doctrines.
I. Pha-boṅ-kha-pa
Byams-pa-bstan-'dzin-'phrin-las-rgya-mtsho, l878–194l.
Rdo rje 'chaṅ Pha boṅ kha pa
dpal bzaṅ pos lam ... English, 1989.
II. Tharchin, Sermey Geshe Lobsang, 1921–.
III. Roach, Michael 1952–.
IV. Title. V. Series.

BQ7645.L3SP47 1995 294.6'444-dc20
95-17797 CIP
ISBN: 978-1-937114-19-0

Printed and bound in the United States of America
Second printing 1999
Third printing 2023

Door To The Diamond Way

TSONGKAPA (1357–1419), also known as Je Rinpoche Lobsang Drakpa, was perhaps the single greatest commentator in the 2,500 year history of Buddhism. He was born in the district of Tsongka in eastern Tibet, and took his first vows at a tender age. As a teenager he had already mastered much of the teachings of Buddhism and was sent by his tutors to the great monastic universities of central Tibet. Here he studied under the leading Buddhist scholars of his day; it is said as well that he enjoyed mystic visions in which he met and learned from different forms of the Buddha himself.

The 18 volumes of Tsongkapa's collected works contain eloquent and incisive commentaries on virtually every major classic of ancient Buddhism, as well as his famed treatises on the "Steps of the Path to Buddhahood." His students, who included the first Dalai Lama of Tibet, contributed hundreds of their own expositions of Buddhist philosophy and practice.

Tsongkapa founded the Great Three monasteries of Tibet, where by custom nearly 25,000 monks have studied the scriptures of Buddhism over the centuries. He also instituted the great Monlam festival, a period of religious study and celebration for the entire Tibetan nation. Tsongkapa passed away in his 62nd year, at his home monastery of Ganden in Lhasa, the capital of Tibet.

PABONGKA RINPOCHE (1878–1941), also known as Jampa Tenzin Trinley Gyatso—or by his Diamond Way name, Dechen Nyingpo—was born into a leading family in the state of Tsang in north-central Tibet. As a boy he entered the Gyalrong House of Sera Mey, one of the colleges of the great Sera Monastic University, and attained the rank of *geshe*, or master of Buddhist philosophy. His powerful public teachings soon made him the leading spiritual figure of his day, and his collected works on every facet of Buddhist thought and practice comprise some 15 volumes. His most famous student was Kyabje Trijang Rinpoche (1901–1981), the junior tutor of the present Dalai Lama. Pabongka Rinpoche passed away at the age of 63 in the Hloka district of south Tibet.

KHEN RINPOCHE, GESHE LOBSANG THARCHIN (1921–2004) was born in Lhasa, and as a boy also entered the Gyalrong House of Sera Mey. He studied under both Pabongka Rinpoche and Kyabje Trijang Rinpoche, and after a rigorous 25-year course in the Buddhist classics was awarded the highest rank of the *geshe* degree. He graduated from the Gyumey Tantric College of Lhasa in 1958 with the position of administrator. In 1959 he escaped the violence in Tibet and in 1974 became abbot of Rashi Gempil Ling, a Kalmuk Mongolian temple in New Jersey, USA. He was the founder of the Mahayana Sutra & Tantra Centers of New Jersey and Washington D.C., and the author of numerous translations of major Buddhist texts, including Pabongka Rinpoche's 3-volume masterpiece, *Liberation in Our Hands*. In 1977 he directed the development of the first computerized Tibetan word processor, and played a leading role in the re-establishment of Sera Mey Monastic College, of which he was a lifetime director. Khen Rinpoche passed away in 2004 at the age of 83.

GESHE MICHAEL ROACH (1952–) graduated with honors from Princeton University and received the Presidential Scholar Medallion from the president of the United States. He is the first westerner in the 600-year history of Sera Mey

Tibetan Monastic University to be awarded the degree of *geshe*. Michael is the founder of the Asian Classics Input Project (now the Asian Legacy Library), which has digitally preserved thousands of ancient Asian books by training and equipping poor people in many countries during the past 35 years. To pay for this work, he helped found Andin International Diamond Corporation of New York, which reached US$250 million in sales and was sold to super-investor Warren Buffett in 2009. *The Diamond Cutter,* his international business bestseller, tells the story of how he used ancient Asian principles for success. Michael founded Diamond Cutter Institute Global for spreading this message to over 100,000 people each year, in more than 30 countries around the world.

Contents

Foreword

Before you start this little book, decide on your motivation for reading it. Think to yourself,

> I want to reach enlightenment as soon as possible. I want to reach it in this very life. And when I do, I will free every living being from every pain of the suffering existence we all live now. Then I will take all these beings up to the level of a Buddha, which is the ultimate state of happiness. This is why I am going to read this book, which shows all the steps to enlightenment.

Take a moment now before you go on. Make sure you have this motivation.

This little book covers absolutely everything that the Buddha ever taught. In Tibet we have a hundred great volumes of the Buddhas' own teachings, translated into Tibetan from Sanskrit, the language of ancient India. And this small book covers all of them.

All the old, great books of Buddhism have but one main goal, and that is to show how any one of us can reach the state of perfect enlightenment. They tell us everything we have to do: how to reach the goal, how to practice, and how to learn. They show us how to begin, they show us how to finish. Everything we need is in those books.

Five hundred years ago in Tibet there came a master monk and teacher, whose name was Tsongkapa the Great. He took these ancient volumes and arranged them into a kind of book known as the *Lam Rim*, which means "Steps of the Path to Enlightenment." Here he laid out all the steps that any of us can go through, one by one in the proper order, if we truly wish to reach enlightenment. He took care to present the steps clearly and simply, yet covering everything that must be done, as we start on the path, and travel along it, and finally reach its end.

The original source work presented here is called the *Source of All My Good*. It is the absolute essence of all the *Lam Rims*, of all the books on the Steps to Enlightenment. The text was written by Tsongkapa himself, and it is named from the opening lines, which read: "The source of all my good is my kind Lama, my Lord."

In the teachings on the Steps this work is also known by another name, something of a secret name, which is *Begging for a Mountain of Blessings*. The word "blessing" here refers to the blessings of all the Buddhas of the universe. "Mountain" comes from a Tibetan word which means a huge pile, a great mass of things all heaped together in one place. The word "begging" is meant to show how much we need and want these blessings.

When we recite this work out loud, then, it's as though we are begging the Buddhas to grant us their blessings, to help us achieve everything from the beginning up to final enlightenment. We are asking them to help us reach all the various paths, all the different levels of knowledge; we are asking for the power of their blessings, we are begging them for help.

Just whom are we asking for help? Normally when we perform the secret Ceremony of the Tenth, we begin with the Practice of Six, followed by the Thousand Angels.[1] Just after that we start this *Source of All My Good*. Therefore we still have in front of us the same holy beings who were there during the Thousand Angels.

---

[1] *Ceremony of the tenth:* This is a regular ceremony for reaching an enlightened Angel, found in the secret teachings of Buddhism, or the "Diamond Way." The Practice of Six and the Thousand Angels are similar.

Sitting in the center, in mid-air before us, is Tsongkapa. Inside his heart is Gentle Voice, or Manjushri, who is the image of all the Buddhas' wisdom. In the heart of Gentle Voice is another holy being, Vajradhara—this is the Keeper of the Diamond, or the Buddha of the secret teachings. His body is blue, and within his own heart is the Sanskrit letter *huung*. This letter is marked with another letter, *mam*.

On Tsongkapa's own right is his disciple Gyaltsab Je, whose full name is Gyaltsab Darma Rinchen (1364–1432). Within this disciple's heart is Loving Eyes, whose Sanskrit name is Avalokiteshvara, and who is the embodiment of all the Buddhas' love. Inside the heart of Loving Eyes is again the Keeper of the Diamond, and in his heart the letter *huung*, marked with a *mam*.

On the other side, to Tsongkapa's left, is his disciple Kedrup Je, whose full name is Kedrup Je Gelek Pelsang (1385–1438). Inside of his heart is the Holder of the Diamond, or Vajrapani, and in the Holder's heart is the Keeper of the Diamond. Within the Keeper's heart is a letter *huung*, marked with a *mam*.

All of these beings are seated in the air in front of you, and they are the ones whom you are asking for their blessing. They are the ones that you are requesting to help you, to grant you every kind of knowledge, from the beginning of the path on up to final enlightenment.

Now I want you to think about something. What is the difference between a Buddha and us? What is it that makes all the Buddhas different from us? And what about you, yourself? You are trying to reach Buddhahood; but what is the difference between all these Buddhas and you? This is a question you must examine, and then the answer will come to you.

What are the Buddhas? First of all, the places where they live are paradise. Pure paradise. The paradises where the Buddhas live are completely pure, they are pure by their very nature, and there is not a single thing about them which is not pure.

Inside themselves too the Buddhas are pure. They have no inner obstacles at all, no bad deeds stored up in them, no problems of any kind. They have none of the problems that are caused by any of the four elements of the physical world, either around them or within them. They have no sickness, no getting old, no death. They do not even have a word for these things where they live. This is why their paradises have names like the "Heaven of Bliss," for the beings there live in the highest happiness there is.

When we think about our own lives then we can see the big difference between Buddhas and us. In one sense we are very fortunate; we have all had the very great fortune to be born as a human being, and we can enjoy that small amount of happiness which human beings sometimes experience. And so sometimes we think we are happy.

But still we have problems, a lot of problems. We have problems all around us, and we have problems inside of us. We have problems that come with the very nature of the kind of life we live. The Buddhas have none of these problems.

Try to think about this difference between the Buddhas and you. Why did you get this book, why are you going to read this book? The main purpose is to reach enlightenment, to gain the highest state of happiness that exists. And to get there you must escape all the sufferings that come with our present kind of life.

To do all this you are going to have to follow some kind of practice. You are going to have to move up through certain levels, certain paths, one by one through a great many different Steps. You will have to go in order, gradually, through each of these Steps. Each higher Step you will have to reach by practicing, and to practice you must learn what to practice. If you never learn what to do, you will never be able to do it.

In this little book you are going to learn what to do. But this is only a preparation for something else.

Generally speaking, this book is all you need. If this is all you ever learn, and if you practice what you learn here, then you will reach enlightenment. But it will take a long time to do so if you restrict yourself to this way, to the way of the open teachings of the Buddha. It will take a very, very long time.

But you want enlightenment, you need it, and you need it now. Why? Because the reason you are reading this book, the whole point of studying these things and reaching these goals, is to help each and every living being. All of them have been your own mother, and the purpose of everything is to help them.

Right now they are suffering, by the very nature of the life we live. Most of them are living in the three lower kinds of birth. Even those who live in one of the higher kinds of birth are suffering too; by the very nature of things, they are in some kind of pain, all the time. Your goal is to save them from this pain; your goal is to help them reach enlightenment, which is absolute happiness. This is why you are studying, this is why you are practicing.

If you only use the way of the open teachings, it will take a long time to reach the goal. But you want the goal now, you want to reach it quickly, because all these living beings around you—all who have been your mother during some lifetime in the past—are suffering in this kind of existence. You cannot stand to have their pain continue, you cannot let them go on suffering so long.

And so you will free them, and you will free them quickly, now. But is there any way to do it so fast? The answer is yes, there is a way, a path that works faster than any other, a path which is very deep and powerful and holy. This is the Diamond Way, the secret path of the Diamond Queen: Vajra Yogini.

To practice this path you must receive an initiation to enter it, and then you must receive her teachings. But before you can do this you must first be granted another initiation, one which will qualify you to study and follow her path. There are four great groups of secret teachings, and to qualify to practice the path of this Angel you must be granted an initiation that belongs to the group which is called the "Unsurpassed." Therefore the most important thing for you to do first is to seek an initiation of the Unsurpassed group.

According to the tradition of the Diamond Queen, the best initiation to prepare yourself for her own initiation and path is the one we call the "Union of the Spheres", or Chakra Sanvara. There are though other initiations of the Unsurpassed group which you can seek if you cannot get this one; for example, there is the initiation of the being known as Frightener, or Bhairava, which is much shorter and easier than the one for the Union of the Spheres, and still qualifies you to take her initiation later.

There is another step you should take too before seeking her initiation. When you go to a college to get an advanced degree, or any degree at all, you must first enter the college. Then you go to classes, do your study, and finally after a number of years you complete all the requirements, and reach your goal. To reach the goal then it is very important that you study and learn, on a constant basis. But to study, and learn, you first have to gain entrance into the college.

It's all the same here. The first thing you have to do is to gain entrance into the Unsurpassed group of the secret teachings of the Buddha. To enter these teachings you have to go through the gate, and this is the initiation. The initiation is the door.

When you take the initiation, you commit yourself to a number of vows. Keeping these vows is like doing your study on a daily basis once you've been allowed to enter the college. In school you have to learn what to study, and then you have to maintain a regular schedule of study. Here in the secret teachings, the vows that you took when you received your initiation are what you have to study: these are what you have to maintain on a regular, daily basis.

To keep the vows, you have to learn all about them. This is why it's essential that after your first initiation you study, in detail, the secret vows, along with the regular vows of morality, and the bodhisattva vows. The very function of these vows, the result of these vows, is very simple. *If you keep them, they produce enlightenment in you.*

Aside from this main function, keeping the vows has another effect as well. In the short run—that is, while you are still on the path, from the very beginning on up to the day you reach the ultimate goal—they help you, they keep you, they preserve you. They make you sweeter and sweeter, more and more pure, every single day you keep them. Everything about you gets better and better: the way you act, the way you think, higher and higher, day by day, month by month.

The vows then are your dear companion, the vows are your devoted helpmate. Vows are not some kind of punishment; the Lama doesn't come to the sacred place of initiation, and say to you, "Well now that you've got the initiation, here are some vows to keep, as a punishment." You must understand all the great good which the vows do for you, and you must learn what they are.

Once you have learned the vows, you must keep them as your daily practice. You should reach a point where, as you look back after some time has passed, you can see progress, you can say to yourself, "A number of years ago, I used to act like that; I had a certain kind of attitude, certain ways of behaving, the limitations of my knowledge were such, and my ability too was only so. Now they have all changed, for the better. Even in the last two years I have changed; no, even in the last year I have changed." You should be able to see for yourself, you should be able to judge, by yourself, whether you are keeping the vows, and how it changes everything about you.

So we are working mainly towards the day when we can receive initiation into the practice of the Diamond Queen. This will allow us to receive her teachings, and then to carry them out. To do this, we will first have to seek any one of the preliminary initiations into the secret teachings of the Unsurpassed group, the highest group of secret teachings.

A person who seeks to be granted an initiation into this highest group should themselves be highest, in the sense that they are highly qualified to receive the initiation. Becoming highly qualified is something that you must do in the proper stages, in certain steps, one by one.

Above I asked you to think about what it was that made Buddhas different from us. In the beginning though all the beings who are Buddhas now were just the same as we are at present. They lived the same kind of suffering life that we pass our days in now, and they did so over millions and millions of years, over many lifetimes.

At some point, though, these beings were able to achieve an excellent life as a human; the same kind that you have now. Within that human life they were able to meet with an excellent spiritual teacher as well. He or she gave them the proper training, and the necessary initiations, and as a result these beings began to get better and better. Finally they achieved enlightenment: they were able to stop all the problems within them and outside of them, everything. If they have been able to practice and achieve this goal, then why can't you? Why not?

And so it is possible for you to become someone who is highly qualified, who is qualified to an unsurpassed degree to take one of the initiations of the Unsurpassed group of the secret teachings. To be qualified to take this initiation, to be a highly qualified practitioner in this sense, means that you must be a practitioner of what we call the *Mahayana*: the Greater Way. This is because all the secret teachings also belong to the greater way; they are in fact the highest teachings and practices of the greater way. You too then will have to be an Unsurpassed practitioner of the greater way. But how do you reach this point?

You must first prepare yourself, with what we call the "shared" practice. The word "shared" means that this preliminary practice is shared by the way of the open teachings, and the greater way, and the way of the secret teachings—all three. It is a practice which all three ways share in common.

Suppose you are planning to construct a very high building, a building with many stories. The most important thing to do first is to build a good foundation, a very strong foundation. If the foundation is strong, then you can build as many stories as you like on top of it.

The little book you have here—*Begging for a Mountain of Blessings,* complete with the commentary of the great Pabongka Rinpoche—presents this foundation. It shows you the practice which is shared by all three ways, and which will prepare you for initiation into the secret teachings. This is the strong foundation upon which you will build your great, high house.

Think about it, and be happy. Take some joy now in what you are about to do. You must realize what a precious opportunity you have in your hands at this very moment, this one good time. Read, and learn, and try not to forget. Try to remember what you learn in this little book, and then try to put it into practice, in your daily life, in a regular way.

By the time you finish this book you should be a different person. The person who picks this book up to read, and the person who sets it down after finishing the last page, should be totally different people. On the inside. You must change: you must change in the way you think, you must change in what you know, in the way you behave all day, in everything about you. Try to change yourself. If you do, then you will win the result of reading this book, of picking it up, and of entering into what it stands for.

Khen Rinpoche
Geshe Lobsang Tharchin

Abbot Emeritus, Sera Mey Tibetan Monastery

Abbot, Rashi Gempil Ling, Kalmuk Buddhist Temple
Freewood Acres, Howell, New Jersey, USA

Je Tsongkapa's Day
December 27, 1994

Some technical notes

❧

The root text here, the *Source of All My Good,* was written by Tsongkapa the Great (1357–1419), perhaps the greatest commentator of Buddhism who ever lived, author of some 10,000 pages in explanation of the early classics of Buddhism, and teacher of many eminent disciples, including the First Dalai Lama. This brief work covers all the necessary stages of the entire path to Buddhahood and is often recited at the beginning of important teachings and high secret rituals. It also forms the final section of *Necklace for the Fortunate,* a popular text used in readying oneself for a Buddhist meditation session.

As will be explained in more detail further on, the text of the *Source of All My Good* is found within a longer work, entitled *Open Door to the Highest Path.* This piece is a supplication to the Lamas of the great lineages of Buddhism: the masters through whom concepts such as the Wish for enlightenment, and the vision of emptiness, have been passed down to us. The importance of the *Door* is indicated by the fact that it appears first in a compendium of 135 briefer titles within the Master's collected works.

The name and role of the work have evolved over the centuries. Je Tsongkapa composed the *Door* in 1402, and by the time of the famous *Path to Bliss,* a presentation on the Steps of the path by His Holiness the First Panchen Lama (1565–1662), it is recommended under its original name for a petition and visualization of the lineage Lamas (see folio 20a, bibliography entry B57).

By the middle part of the 18th century the *Door's* central section, itself a concise yet complete presentation of the Steps, has become the subject of a number of philosophical commentaries, under the name of the *Source of All My Good* (a phrase taken from the first line of the text). By this time too, the work is being referred to by the name of *Begging for a Mountain of Blessings* (see bibliography entry B69). It is also recommended throughout this period as a component in the six standard practices used to prepare for a meditation session.

Other commentaries or works based on the *Source* include those of the following authors:

> Akuching Drungchen Sherab Gyatso (b. 1803), at bibliography entry B74
>
> Gushri Kachupa Mergen Kenpo Lobsang Tsepel (b. about 1760), entries B64 and B63
>
> Gyal Kenpo Drakpa Gyaltsen (1762–1837), entry B12
>
> His Holiness the Sixth Panchen Lama, Lobsang Tupten Chukyi Nyima (1883–1937), entry B61
>
> Je Lodro Gyatso (1851–1930), ed. by Gyal Kentrul Kelsang Drakpa Gyatso (b. 1880), entry B54
>
> Jikme Samten (19th century), entry B25
>
> Kalka Damtsik Dorje (1781–1855), entry B44
>
> Kirti Lobsang Trinley (1849–1905), entries B1 and B2
>
> Lumbum Sherab Gyatso (1884–1968), entry B73
>
> Ngawang Yeshe Tupten Rabjampa (19th century), entry B19

Shangton Tenpa Gyatso Pel Sangpo (1825–1897),
   entry B40

Shasana Dipam (n. d.), entry B76

Tsechok Ling Yeshe Gyaltsen (1713–1793), entry B69

Explanations of the six preliminary practices are also a rich source of commentary upon the *Source*. Pabongka Rinpoche himself gives a profound interpretation of the text in two such works (at f. 80b, entry B51, and ff. 36a–39a, entry B49). He includes all the original verses in a recitation text based on the Fifth Dalai Lama's presentation of the Steps (see ff. 9b–11a, entry B50, and entry B21).

He also mentions using them as the basis of a review meditation in his masterpiece on the Steps to Buddhahood entitled *A Gift of Liberation, Thrust into Our Hands* (on folio 21a, entry B48). And it was his own precious teacher, Dakpo Lama Jampel Hlundrup (1845–1919), who attached the work to the *Necklace* mentioned above (entry B23).

Other commentaries on the six practices which include explanations of the *Source* have been written by the following masters:

Akya Yangchen Gaway Lodru (1740–1827),
   at entry B65

Keutsang Lobsang Jamyang Monlam
   (b. 1689), entry B3

Tsechok Ling Yeshe Gyaltsen (1713–1793),
   entry B70

The Second Jamyang Shepa, Konchok Jikme
   Wangpo (1728–1791), entry B4

One very interesting additional work is another *Open Door to the Highest Path,* written by Tsechok Ling Yeshe Gyaltsen (1713–1793). The title is the same as that of Je Tsongkapa's original piece because the author undertakes to extend Tsongkapa's supplication to later Lamas of the lineage, in order to include the great teachers beginning from Je Tsongkapa himself. This addendum begins at f. 4a, entry B68.

Incidentally, the very expression "source of all my good" (in the Tibetan form of *yon-tan gyi gzhi-rten*) is used very early on in Buddhist literature. The phrase in Sanskrit appears in the *Letter to a Friend,* written by the realized being Nagarjuna some seventeen centuries ago. Here it refers to the practice of morality which, like proper reliance upon a Lama, acts to provide us with all good things. (See entry S19, f. 41a; entry E8, p. 38; and entry B48, folio 284b.)

❖ ❖ ❖

Striking a balance in translation between the needs of the average reader and more experienced specialists is always difficult. For this translation we have observed the following conventions.

We have tried not to leave in the text foreign words that might prove a stumbling block to the average English-speaking audience. Proper names where the words of the name could be considered to have symbolic significance have been translated for the benefit of the average reader, who would otherwise miss this symbolism. Since these translated names will be unfamiliar to the specialist, we have provided an appendix listing the English names with their Tibetan and Sanskrit equivalents.

With some hesitance we have chosen to use a number of English spiritual terms for words in the original Asian languages which are close to them in meaning, and for which no exact English word exists; this was again to avoid using foreign words unfamiliar to the average reader. We would like to note a few of these words here.

The word "angel" is used for the Tibetan *lha* or *mkha'-'gro*, and the like. The reader should be aware though that the idea is not of a messenger from God, but rather of a specialized form that an Enlightened Being takes in order to perform specific sacred tasks, including personal spiritual contact with normal humans. The words "heaven" and "paradise" are used for the Tibetan *dag-zhing* and similar expressions. These refer not to a perfect place beyond the sky where good people go after their death, but rather to a state of spiritual perfection, attainable at any point in a person's life, wherein one's own being and the place where they live consist of total bliss, free of every form of suffering. Further such terms will be understood from their context.

Other personal names, words for plants or such objects that have no common English equivalent, and the like have been left in a simplified pronunciation which approximates the sound of the original foreign word, but without the use of diacritical marks which are not found in normal English writing. Again, this is to help the ordinary English reader. The vowels for words that appear in the simplified pronunciation should be pronounced as follows: *a* as the one in "all," *e* as the one in "yet," *i* as the one in "bit," *o* as the one in "hoe," and *u* as the one in "Luke."

During the course of his teaching Pabongka Rinpoche quotes a great number of profound sources. We have located nearly all of these references, and the specialists—in reward for their patience with our other simplifications—are provided with full original spellings and bibliographic data that will allow them to find and enjoy reading the various source texts in the original language.

Acknowledgements

Finally, we would like to express our sincere thanks to Ms. Barbara Taylor for her efforts in preparing the original text for publication. The new edition of 2023 is the result of hard work by a devoted team of friends & colleagues.

First we would like to thank Rosa van Grieken and Ven. Elizabeth van der Pas of the Diamond Cutter Press (DCP), for their tireless work in preparing this and many other valuable books for publication. We would also like to thank Dr. Artemus Engle of the Mahayana Sutra & Tantra Press (MSTP) for keeping this book in print for the many years since its first publication, and for granting DCP permission to reprint it here.

The director of the Diamond Cutter Classics translation team, Nicholas Lashaw, and assistant director Ben Kramer spent many hours updating the bibliography and footnotes so that the ancient texts listed can now easily be located by readers in the Asian Legacy Library (ALL) database of searchable classics of Asia. We would like to express our thanks to ALL director John Brady and his team for their many years of searching out and preserving these classics; their work is invaluable for our own translation efforts. The Buddhist Digital Resource Center (BDRC), along with director Jann Ronis have also offered us unstinting help in locating copies of necessary texts.

Special thanks are due to the kind & generous financial sponsors of the ALL and DCC efforts. You know who you are, and we love you! Without your trust and support we would be able to accomplish very little.

Our DCP editing team, led by the tireless Bets Greer, with the great help of Anatole Nguyen and Rebecca Vinacour, has devoted countless hours to the deep labor of checking and rechecking every single detail of this and all of our publications. And finally of course none of this labor could have been possible without the selfless efforts of our teachers—especially Khen Rinpoche Geshe Lobsang Tharchin (1921–2004)—and all of those who over the centuries have devoted their lives to keeping this wisdom healthy and alive in this world.

Door to the Diamond Way
The Mountain of Blessings

Herein contained is a book named
*Opening Your Eyes to What You Should Keep,
and What You Should Give Up.*[2]

It consists of a brief series of notes that were taken
at a teaching delivered by the Lord of the Secret World,
Vajradhara, the Keeper of the Diamond,
the Good and Glorious Pabongka.[3]

The teaching was a profound explanation
of the text known as
the *Source of All My Good,*
a work which is the distilled essence of
the Steps of the path to Buddhahood.

---

[2] *Opening Your Eyes:* The edition used for this translation is a woodblock print of 27 folios on handmade Tibetan paper held in the private collection of the venerable Geshe Lobsang Thardo, from the Gyalrong College of Sera Mey Tibetan Monastic University, South India. The copy was presented to him personally by the Third Pabongka Rinpoche, the Ven. Geshe Lobsang Tupten Trinley Kunkyab. Another copy is listed in the catalog to the library of His Holiness Trijang Rinpoche, the late tutor of the present Dalai Lama. The text is somewhat rare, and was not included in the standard edition of Pabongka Rinpoche's collected works. See bibliography entry B46.

[3] *The Good and Glorious Pabongka:* Refers to the first Pabongka Rinpoche (1878–1941), whose full monk's name was Jampa Tenzin Trinley Gyatso. He was the foremost Buddhist teacher of his era, and renowned for his ability to convey the deepest concepts of Buddhism to the common man in popular public teachings. For a full biography in English, refer to the introduction of *The Principal Teachings of Buddhism,* bibliography entry E9.

❖ ❖ ❖

In deepest reverence, expressed through all three doors,[4]
I bow to the lotus feet of the person who is the Essence
of Great Bliss, the Venerated One, the Holy Lama,
Lobsang the Great, Lord of All Buddhas,
the One Who Keeps the Diamond.[5]

---

[4] *All three doors:* The three ways in which we can express ourselves—in action, speech, or thought. A typical presentation of the three appears in the works on Higher Knowledge (*Abhidharma*); see for example Choney Lama Drakpa Shedrup (1675–1748), entry B10, folio 123a.

[5] *The person who is the Essence of Great Bliss:* Another name for Pabongka Rinpoche, describing his mastery of the secret teachings of Buddhism. The additional names that follow indicate that the Rinpoche embodies Je Tsongkapa, Shakyamuni Buddha, and the form that Lord Buddha takes to deliver the secret Word.

How the Teaching Was Given

Here I will give just a brief account of a wonderful teaching bestowed upon us by the One, the Lord of the Secret World, the Savior of His Followers, and the Keeper of the Diamond: Pabongka Rinpoche, whose kindness knows no match.

His teaching was a profound clarification of the one and only highway used by each and every Victor of the past, present, and future to reach the highest goals; the Steps on the path to Buddhahood, its very essence distilled; the inner nectar of the instructions imparted by our Father, the Lord, the Buddha himself come again; and the ultimate elixir extracted from the highest of words, the Speech of the Enlightened Ones: that is to say, the work known to us as the Source of All My Good, *also called* Begging for a Mountain of Blessings.[6]

As he began the teaching, the Lord himself led us in reciting the Essence of Wisdom, *and then the prayer of Sinha Mukhi—the Angel with the Face of a Lion, from the part where we ward off any evil that might disrupt the teaching, all the way up to the words "May goodness come to be," in the way we usually do them.*

Then in turns we took the lead, sounding out in unison the various verses that include the words "Virtues perfected finally"; and "Loving One, Avalokiteshvara, with Asanga"; and "Gentle Voice, Manjushri, with the one who destroyed the extremes of being

---

[6] *Mountain of Blessings:* The concept of a blessing in Buddhism refers to a specific process through which a disciple's ability to achieve spiritual goals is altered, enhanced, through a true request to a Lama for his or her blessing. Pabongka Rinpoche himself describes this in his famed *Gift of Liberation,* entry B48, ff. 90a–90b.

and not"; and "The one of great compassion"; and "Teaching what to learn, to reach"; and "Founder from the Land of Snow"; and "All three places of refuge in one"; and "The constellations of the highest of words"; and "In all my lives."

The lead then went to the chanting master, who guided us in the offering of the mandala, beginning with "The great Earth, filled with the smell of incense," and on through "Atop a lion throne in the space before me," as well as "Sponges of the sky, made of most excellent knowledge and love," along with the lines that begin with idam guru.

The lead returned to the Keeper of the Diamond, who deigned to direct us thrice through the prayer for taking refuge and developing the Wish for enlightenment, the one that includes the words "To the Buddha, Dharma, and Sangha." Here finally the lord himself bespoke the verses containing the lines "Pleasure beings and those near so," along with "In the language of pleasure beings" and the rest.[7]

---

[7] *Language of pleasure beings:* These and the other lines belong to selected verses which are recited by tradition at the start of a major teaching, in order for both teacher and listener to begin with the proper motivation; to formally request the teaching; to prevent obstacles that might disrupt the teaching; and so on.

The verses can be found in standard prayer books for Tibetan Buddhist monasteries, such as the one listed in bibliography entry B81. Their locations here are as follows: *Essence of Wisdom* (the famous *Heart Sutra*, for preventing obstacles), p. 346; *Angel with the Face of a Lion* (also for preventing obstacles), p. 367; "Virtues perfected" (opening lines of Je Tsongkapa's brief *Stages of the Path* and an obeisance to Lord Buddha), p. 270; "Loving One" (these and following common verses of obeisance and the offering of bathing to the lineage Lamas), p. 7; "Gentle Voice," p. 7; "The one of great compassion," p. 7; "Teaching what to learn, to reach," p. 7; "Founder from the Land of Snows," p. 141 of entry B23; "All three places" (these last two also common graces), p. 143; "The constellations," p. 8; "In all my lives" (also attached to the *Mountain of Blessings*), p. 125; "The great Earth" (the shorter offering of the mandala), p. 12; "Atop a lion throne" (from a prayer of devotion to Je Tsongkapa), p. 123; "Sponges of the sky" (a request for teaching from the famous *Offering to Lamas*), p. 123; *"Idam guru"* (final words of the mandala offering), p. 12; "To the Buddha" (the well-known formula for taking refuge and developing the Wish for enlightenment), p. 1; "Pleasure beings" (an obeisance to Tara, the Angel of Liberation), p. 336; and "Language of pleasure beings" (a prayer to teach in all the world's languages), p. 308.

The Preliminaries

I. Why the Steps?

"And so we begin," said the Lama.

Let me remind you, he said, of those lines by the King of the Dharma of all three realms—Tsongkapa the Great; the ones that mention "This life of spiritual leisure, more precious than a jewel that can give you whatever you wish for."[8] The refrain throughout these verses reads: "Those of you who wish for freedom should seek to master this, as I have done." You and I have lived in this circle of suffering life forever; and there is not a single form of life, in any of the six realms of pain, that we have not already lived.

In these lives we have suffered, and enjoyed the occasional short-lived pleasure, wandering aimlessly from that high level known as the "Peak of Existence," then down to the lowest hell, "Torment with No Respite," then back, and back again. We have lived this way for time with no beginning, and yet we have never gotten any meaning out of it; the time has slipped away from us useless, senseless, empty. And so still we are here, circling up & down in the three realms of the wheel of life, and certain we are to continue the round.

At some point in days gone by, you and I through sheer good luck were taken for some brief moments under the care of a Lama, or the Three Jewels, and so were able to gather together some bit of pure and powerful karma. The force of this karma, I will admit, has allowed us to gain, just this once, the present life we enjoy—full of the various leisures

---

[8] *This life of spiritual leisure:* Found in the Master's *Songs of My Spiritual Life,* f. 56a, entry B30.

and fortunes, free of the problems that come when we lack the conditions that allow a proper spiritual practice.

I will admit as well that everything we need has come together for us this time: we have a Lama, we have some Dharma to practice, we have every favorable condition that we need. And so the capability to follow the spiritual path is something we now hold in our own two hands. Yet suppose we fail; suppose that we find ourselves unable to achieve the ultimate goal of the infinite lives we have led.

Beyond a doubt then we will fall back again to the births where we have no chance for Dharma. And when we fall it matters not where we fall; wherever we fall in a birth without the Dharma, our life can never be anything but pain.

The way to avoid ever taking another birth where we have no chance for Dharma is to practice the Dharma purely now; there is no better way at all. And our practice must start this minute; you will die, you must die, it is certain you will die. But you've no idea when. And what will happen after that?

Whatever we do now decides where we go then: if we do good, it will throw us forth into one of the better births; if we do wrong, it will throw us to a birth of misery. So suppose we fail to practice; suppose we die in the middle of our present evil way of life. It is only fitting then that we should go right where we belong: to these very births of misery.

We must then for the short term go for shelter to the Three Jewels, to keep ourselves from a birth in the lower realms. We must as well open up and admit the things we have done wrong before, and restrain ourselves in the future. To do so we must make strong and heartfelt use of the four forces[9]

---

[9] *The four forces:* Buddhism teaches that there are four antidote forces, which together can remove the power or karma of any bad deed. The "basis" force consists of thinking who it is that was offended by your deed, and who it is you will rely on to clear yourself of it. The "destruction" force is an intense feeling of shame and regret for the deed, which will certainly return to hurt you. The "reverse" force is to turn yourself away from doing that kind of deed

that counteract the power of the wrong. We must too put all our effort into taking up even the smallest virtue, and giving up even the slightest harms we commit against others.

If in addition to all this we are able to follow perfectly the path of the three extraordinary trainings,[10] then we ourselves will come to be free of each and every fear of the circle of suffering life. But it's not enough if it is only you who escapes the circle, for we must recall the words of the Master Chandragomi:

> Even a cow knows how
> To take care of themselves,
> To eat a few clumps of grass
> They easily come across;
>
> Even the beast can merrily drink
> From a pool of water they find
> As bitter thirst torments them.
>
> But think now what it is
> To put your whole heart
> Into taking care of others;
>
> This is glory,
> This is a park of pleasure,
> This is the ultimate.

---

again. The "counteragent" force is to undertake some spiritual practice—confession, meditation, or any good deed—to offset the power of the wrong. See Pabongka Rinpoche, entry B48, ff. 109a–113b, 246a–248a.

[10] *Three extraordinary trainings:* That is, extraordinary morality, extraordinary concentration, and extraordinary wisdom. Each one acts as a support for the next. A thorough discussion of the three is found in the monastic textbooks on the perfection of wisdom; see for example *An Overview of the Perfection of Wisdom* by Kedrup Tenpa Dargye (1493–1568), f. 24a*ff.*, Vol. 1, entry B42.

The Sun
Climbs aboard his fantastic chariot,
Flies across the sky,
Lights up all the world.

The Earth
Raises up her mighty arms,
Bears the load,
Holds up all humankind.

And so is the way
Of those great beings
Who wish nothing
For themselves,

Their lives devoted
To a single song:
The well-being and the happiness
Of every living thing.[11]

We must do as the verses say: we must distinguish ourselves from common animals, we must find that great courage of heart to accomplish the goals of all other sentient kind. And there is a good reason why we should.

Every single creature in the universe has been our father, and been our mother, not once, but more times than numbers can count. And there is not a one who when they served as our parent did not shower us with every deep kindness, over and over again.

Suppose then I were to forget their kindness, and give no thought to returning it. This would truly be an evil way to

---

[11] *Happiness of every living thing:* The quotation is from the *Letter to a Student,* written by Master Chandragomi in the 10th century. It appears as well in Je Tsongkapa's greater *Steps to the Path* and the first Panchen Lama's *Path of Ease.* See f. 52a, bibliography entry S13; f. 183b, entry B26; and f. 17b, entry B57, respectively.

act, the way of a person without a conscience, of one who had no shame. For the *Verses of Drumsong, King of the Serpentines*, says as well:

> The sea is not my problem,
> My task is not the mountains,
> My job is not the earth;
>
> My calling's rather to attend
> That I should never fail
> Repaying kindness granted me.[12]

So too say the lines,

> A kindness returned is goodness,
> And evil is kindness unreturned.[13]

Think: everything we have now, from this precious human body on up, has come to us through the kindness of other living beings. And so it is now that we must repay them. The repayment must begin here, in these circumstances, while I am able, while I possess this perfect form for the practice of the Dharma.

If now I cannot accomplish this great goal, if all I have gained is wasted, then there is little point in claiming to work for every living being: it is little likely that I myself will be able even to reach the higher realms of suffering life again.

---

[12] *The sea is not my problem:* The quotation is found in a teaching of the Buddha, where he recounts the story of a serpentine king, as an admonition to his monks for quarreling. The popular lines are also found in the *Greater Steps* of Je Tsongkapa; the *Word of Gentle Voice* by the Fifth Dalai Lama (1617–1682); the *Easy Path to Omniscience* by Changkya Ngawang Chunden (1642–1714); and the *Steps of the Teaching,* a massive prototype for the *Greater Steps* composed by Geshe Drolungpa (c. 1100). See respectively f. 316a, entry S29; f. 197a, entry B26; f. 53b, entry B21; f. 124a, entry B18; and f. 170a, entry B55.

[13] This appears to be a proverb rather than a scriptural reference; the *Steps of the Teaching* expresses a very similar sentiment at f. 295a, entry B55.

What is the way then to pay this kindness back? No way would be higher than to see to it that every living creature has every happiness there is, and that every living creature is free of every pain which exists. And I will do it! Raise these thoughts of love and compassion up in your heart—bring them on fiercely.

And then you must resolve to take the load upon yourself: "I will rely on no one else in this work; it should be I, and I alone who brings every happiness to every being, and frees each one from every pain."

Yet the ability to perform this noble task is had only by a single being: only by a Buddha, there's no one else at all who can do it. If for the sole purpose of all other living creatures I can reach the state of a Buddha, then I can fulfill completely both of the ultimate goals,[14] and so by the way achieve everything I ever needed as well.

If this is not the way I go—if instead I achieve a lower nirvana, and become one of those foe destroyers they call a listener, or a "self-made buddha,"[15] then I cannot achieve

---

[14] *Both of the ultimate goals:* Refers to the final culmination of one's own goals and the ability to help others achieve theirs—two qualities possessed only by a Buddha. Several important discussions of the ultimate goals are found in treatises on Master Dharmakirti's *Commentary on Accurate Perception*, composed in the 7th century. The first is included in the explanation of the opening lines of this work itself, where the Buddha's qualities are extolled. The second comes in the second chapter, as Master Dharmakirti explains the praise of the Buddha in Master Dignaga's original treatise. See ACIP digital versions of the root text, f. 94b and f. 112b*ff.*, entry S15, as well as the famed commentary by Je Tsongkapa's student Gyaltsab Je (1364–1432), ff. 3b–4b and sections starting at 127b, 141b, and 166b, entry B17.

[15] *One of those foe destroyers:* "Foe destroyer" is a term used to refer to those who have achieved nirvana, since—as Geshe Drolungpa notes in his *Steps of the Teaching*—they have permanently destroyed the foe of the negative emotions (see f. 374b, entry B55). "Listeners" and "self-made buddhas" here refer to persons who have achieved nirvana but have not yet entered the higher way, the way of the bodhisattvas, where they work to become fully enlightened Buddhas in order to liberate all living beings.

"Listeners" are so called because they can listen to the teachings of the higher way, and even relate them to others, but do not actually put them into

all that I need myself, and can accomplish no more than a shadow of what others need from me.

And so I must reach the state of a Buddha, the One who has come to the final end where their own and other's needs are perfectly filled. To do so, I must know how. To know how, I must learn how. I will begin with the Dharma of this very teaching, and others like it; I will follow these instructions well, and I will come to the state of Buddhahood itself.

Think these thoughts to yourself, here as our teaching starts, for they are the greater way's Wish for Buddhahood. At the very least, you must try to imitate this line of thinking; even if you cannot do the real thing, let these thoughts dwell in your heart all through the teaching that you are about to hear.

And what is the teaching that you are to hear? It was spoken by our Gentle Savior, by the Lama, the Great Tsongkapa, at Yangun—the hermitage of the Victor. This was at the monastery of Radreng, standing to the north, at the foot of a great crag of rock shaped like the mouth of a lion.[16]

---

practice themselves. "Self-made buddhas" are not real Buddhas, but have only achieved nirvana, and are "self-made" only insofar as they have reached this state without relying on a spiritual teacher in the present life, although they have had countless such teachers in their past lives. See ACIP digital versions of Kedrup Tenpa Dargye, ff. 79b–80a, Vol. 1, entry B42; Je Tsongkapa, f. 5a, entry B32; and the *Great Dictionary*, p. 2659, entry B80.

[16] *The great monastery of Radreng:* The chain of events surrounding the composition of the *Mountain of Blessings* is extraordinary; it shows how this brief supplication played a pivotal role in Je Tsongkapa's spiritual life, and in the history of Buddhist literature.

Much of what Je Tsongkapa wrote is said to have been dictated to him by Manjushri, Gentle Voice, who is the wisdom of all Enlightened Beings combined in the form of a single angel. Je Tsongkapa began to enjoy communication with Gentle Voice in his early thirties. At this point he was still incapable of seeing the angel directly himself, but was able to pose questions to him through a mediator, a lama named Umapa.

Je Tsongkapa's *Secret Biography*, a work by his close disciple Kedrup Je (1385–1438), describes important events of the Master's inner life. Here we read the details of an early exchange between Je Tsongkapa and Gentle Voice, with Lama Umapa acting as go-between. Je Rinpoche poses questions, and the angel begins his answer by clarifying a whole range of thorny issues concerning the subject of emptiness. Next he moves on to illuminate a number of difficult points in the secret teachings. Then he pauses, and Je Rinpoche says: "But wait, there are still more questions I must ask, more points I cannot grasp."

And Gentle Voice replies,

> Do not forget the answers I have already given you today. Go now and write a record of them. There are three practices then you must undertake, all three together, and you must devote yourself to them with an unquenchable passion.
>
> First you must come to see that your Lama and your high secret Angel are one and the same. You must make supplication to them, and try to reach them.
>
> Secondly you must make constant and perfect efforts in the two-fold practice of collecting the energy of good deeds, and purifying yourself of the force of evil deeds.
>
> Thirdly you must use the power of your intellect to investigate the true meaning of the great books of Buddhism, and then you must contemplate this meaning deeply.
>
> Follow these three practices, keep them up over a long period of time. There will come a day—it is not far off—when the seed I have planted within you in this hour will flower. And then you will understand all, perfectly. (See bibliography entry B8, f. 3a.)

Throughout his life Je Tsongkapa followed all three practices, but the particular attention he paid to supplication, to prayers for the blessings of perfected beings—Buddhas and Lamas—is strikingly evident in records of his writings, and throughout his various biographies.

It is one such supplication which leads to our present work, the *Mountain of Blessings*. The time is the summer of 1402, in the forty-sixth year of the Master's life. Having spent a fruitful summer at the Temple of Ar with his close teacher and disciple, the Sakya sage Jetsun Rendawa, Je Tsongkapa then travels to Radreng ("to the north" of Lhasa). He has been there once before, attracted to the great monastery so full of the history of two of Tibetan Buddhism's founding fathers: Atisha, the Lord, and his spiritual son Dromtun Je (the "Victor" mentioned in the text). This connection is described by Kedrup Je in his longer biography (entry B7, f. 39b).

At Radreng, Je Tsongkapa goes into solitude at the foot of the lion crag. Above his quarters is a statue of the Lord himself, Atisha. One day the Master kneels before the image, in keeping with the words of Gentle Voice himself, and makes a supplication to the Lamas of the past.

The prayer that Je Tsongkapa made that day is still extant, and can be found in his collected works under the name of *Door to the Highest Path.* The petition is directed to the Lamas of the instructions on the Steps to Buddhahood, and divides broadly into three parts.

The first part is a request to the teachers of the lineage of the Wish for enlightenment, beginning with the Buddha himself, and continuing on through Loving One; the Indian master Asanga; and then on down to the great Tibetan lamas of Je Rinpoche's own time. The third part is a similar prayer, to the teachers of the lineage of the Realization of emptiness—again starting with Lord Buddha, and passing down through Gentle Voice, the incomparable Nagarjuna, and later generations.

The second part, between these two, is none other than the *Mountain of Blessings,* the *Source of All My Good.* Je Tsongkapa ends his prayer, and suddenly goes into a vision, one which, according to the *Great Biography* of Gyalwang Lobsang Trinley Namgyal (about 1840), continues on and off for an entire month. (See entry B62, pp. 266–271.) He sees all the lineage Lamas face-to-face, and receives a momentous boon from one in particular.

The scene is recorded in a standard set of fifteen scroll paintings of the Master's life known as *The Tsongkapa Eighty;* our team has translated this work in an extensive, illustrated book known as *King of the Dharma* (see Section 108, p. 369; entry E6). We find the following description of the event on the scroll, in this work of the great Jamyang Shepay Dorje (1648–1721):

> And then Lord Atisha came to the Master, and placed his hand on his head, and said to him, "Do mighty deeds on behalf of the Teachings, and then I myself will assist you in reaching the goal of Enlightenment, and filling the needs of every living being." (Entry B24, ff. 13a–13b.)

Immediately after the vision, Je Tsongkapa is approached by scores of learned disciples, who entreat him to write a detailed account of how to reach perfection. Flush with Lord Atisha's promise, the Master goes into retreat, and there at Radreng completes his masterwork—the *Lam Rim Chenmo,* or *Greater Steps of the Path to Buddhahood*—the most famous book in all of Tibetan Buddhism.

His understanding is now complete, and the seed planted by Gentle Voice has flowered as foretold, for Je Tsongkapa has heeded the angel's advice by composing this perfect supplication: the *Mountain of Blessings.* This power of the prayer has been recognized throughout generations of lamas since, and explains why it is used as a preparation for the secret practices. As the final lines of the present explanation of the work reveal, it too has been imparted by Pabongka Rinpoche as a preliminary to a tantric initiation.

The Lord imparted these vital instructions to his disciples there, acting only for the good of living beings and the Buddha's Word. The title of the text he spoke is the *Source of All My Good;* it is also known by another name, *Begging for a Mountain of Blessings.*

This is a work of the kind we call the "Steps to Buddhahood"; books like this contain within themselves each and every crucial point in all the open and secret teachings of Buddhism. They present these points without the slightest error, from the very beginning to the very end: from finding and serving a spiritual guide on up to the perfect secret Union, where there is nothing more to learn.

These teachings on the Steps are the pure essence of everything that all the victorious Buddhas have ever spoken, the sum rolled into one. They are the one and only form of the Teaching that embodies all of the greater way; they are the point of the tip of the highest, matchless peak.

Our Lord Lama, in his work entitled *Songs of My Spiritual Life,* says,

> When within yourself you've developed
> The path that is shared,
> The one that's needed
> For both the highest paths...[17]

What he means is that, speaking in a general way, this instruction on the Steps to Buddhahood is one that you could never do without, whether you are practicing the open or the secret teachings of Buddhism. To put it more specifically, the Great Fifth of the Dalai Lamas has said,

---

[17] *Both the highest paths:* Refers to the paths of the open and the secret teachings of Buddhism. The path which is "shared" by the two consists of the realizations of the Steps to Buddhahood, since these are necessary for success in both the open and the secret ways. The quotation is from Je Rinpoche's *Briefer Steps of the Path* (entry B30, f. 57b).

Everybody talks of it,
The Secret Word, The Most Profound,
Essential thread
In the River of Dharma
For those of the great capacity;

But try it before
Your mind is trained
In the path that both them share,
Climb atop a mighty elephant
Still wild, and not yet tamed;

And you will only lose
Yourself.[18]

It is absolutely vital then, for anyone with hopes of entering the door that leads to the way of the Secret Word, that you train your mind first in this path shared by both the open and secret teachings.

Now there is a reason why this text is known as "Begging for a Mountain of Blessings." As we recite it we are *entreating* our Lama to grant us, in one big *pile* or mountain, each and every spiritual realization: from finding and following a spiritual guide as we should, on up to the perfect Union. And we are asking that they do so in the form of a *personal blessing* from themselves. As the spiritual friend Tunpa has spoken,

---

[18] *You will only lose yourself*: See f. 6b of his *Lake That Reflects a Million Moons* (entry B20). The Fifth Dalai Lama, His Holiness Ngawang Lobsang Gyatso (1617–1682), was an extraordinary scholar and organizer of Buddhism, so much so that he is referred to in Tibet simply as the "Great Fifth." He is known for bringing the famous Potala Palace to its present form; for his writings on a broad range of philosophical and secular subjects; and for his special visions and mastery of the secret teachings.

The ability to wrap the totality of the teachings
into one is a special skill of my Lama's—for the
Father, nothing is not a teaching.[19]

He has said as well that:

His wondrous word is all three the collections,
Advice adorned by teachings of three scopes,
A gold and jewel rosary of the Keepers,
Meaningful to all who read its beads.[20]

---

[19] *Nothing is not a teaching:* The line is found in a piece entitled *Dromtun Je's
Latter Epistle to Shangtrang Kaberchung,* which at this point is quoting single
lines by Dromtun Je that also appear in the *Greater Steps* of Je Tsongkapa (see
f. 46b, entry B16). Here and in the *Gift* of Pabongka Rinpoche, the quotation is
used to emphasize how practitioners at an advanced level see all the Buddhist
teachings as being totally consistent internally; refer to f. 11a, entry B26, and
ff. 43b-44a, entry B48.

None of these three occurrences of the line includes the part beginning with
"for the Father," nor is it present in the quotation as found in the text on the
Steps by the Great Fifth Dalai Lama at f. 4b, entry B21. The sense though
matches the context of the *Selections* and the standard use of the reference.

The words translated here as "wrapping the totality of the teachings
into one" can be read in a number of different ways, as noted by Pabongka
Rinpoche himself in the *Gift,* at the folios listed above. Literally the text speaks
of "carrying all the teachings as a square," which the Rinpoche interprets
finally as referring to how a square Tibetan carpet automatically comes with
four corners. That is, any teaching on the Steps of the path automatically
contains in it all the teachings of the Buddha, providing an abbreviated
presentation that any one of us can use to achieve total enlightenment.

The great Drom Tunpa (1005–1064), full name Dromtun Gyalway Jungney,
was the most famed disciple of Lord Atisha (982–1052), himself the illustrious
progenitor of the teaching on the Steps in Tibet. Drom Tunpa also founded the
great monastery of Radreng, which is where Je Tsongkapa wrote the *Mountain
of Blessings.*

[20] *A gold and jewel rosary:* Original source of quotation not found; it also occurs
within multiple other works, such as Pabongka Rinpoche's commentary to the
Three Principal Paths. See f. 8a, entry B47 (English at p. 55, entry E9). One early
citation of it may be found in the spiritual history of the Kadampa by Panchen
Sunam Drakpa (1478–1554); see ff. 32b–33a, entry B78. The American scholar
Artemus Engle has traced the lines to a work whose title he translates as *The
Shorter Treatise on the Sevenfold Tradition of Deities and Teachings (Lha chos bdun-
ldan chung-ba),* but a copy has not yet been located (personal communication,
May 2023).

Geshe Tunpa is describing here what our Lord Lama has spoken in all his presentations of the Steps of the path, both the brief and more detailed: that these very Steps are far superior to every other form of instruction, by virtue of their three extraordinary qualities, and four different kinds of greatness.[21] They contain each and every crucial point in

---

The "three scopes" refer to three levels of motivation for practicing the Steps of the path: to escape the three lower rebirths, to escape all suffering, and to achieve total enlightenment in order to help all living beings. The "three collections" are the three sections of the Buddha's word: the "collection of vowed morality," dedicated chiefly to the extraordinary training of morality; the "collection of sutra," concerned primarily with the training of concentration; and the "collection of higher knowledge," devoted to the training of wisdom. See Pabongka Rinpoche's *Gift of Liberation*, f. 17b, entry B48; and Kedrup Tenpa Dargye's *Overview of the Perfection of Wisdom* at f. 25a, Vol. 1, entry B42.

The "Keepers" are explained below at footnote 29 (*The older Keepers of the Word*, page 38).

[21] *These Steps are far superior*: Pabongka Rinpoche himself, in *A Gift of Liberation*, describes the "three extraordinary qualities" as follows. The works on the Steps to the path are (1) totally complete, with nothing left out, for they present in a concise way the entire contents of the teachings of the Buddha, both open and secret. They are (2) easily put into practice, for their main point is to explain the various steps for taming the mind. Finally, they are (3) vastly superior to other teachings, since they consist of the systems of the two great founders—Arya Nagarjuna and Master Asanga—enhanced by the instructions of Lama Vidyakokila and Lama Serlingpa, respectively. See ff. 48b–50b, entry B48.

Arya Nagarjuna (200AD) is known as the founder of the teachings on emptiness, and Master Asanga (350AD) as that of the teachings on bodhisattva activities. The lineages come down respectively to Lama Vidyakokila and Lama Serlingpa, and then combine in their illustrious student, Lord Atisha (982–1054). The Lord's full name is Dipamkara Shri Jnyana; it was he who brought the teachings of the Steps of the path to Tibet, and who authored the *Lamp for the Path*, a prototype text of this genre. See entry S1.

The "four kinds of greatness" also appear in Pabongka Rinpoche's *Gift*. The teachings on the Steps of the path are great in that (1) they allow a person to realize that every single teaching of Buddhism is consistent with every other one. They bring a person to a level where (2) he or she sees everything the Buddha taught as something that can be put into personal practice. They (3) help a person to discern with ease the true intention of the Buddha in each of his teachings, and thereby (4) automatically protect us from making the Great Mistake; that is, the error of thinking that some of the Buddha's instructions are better, and some worse. See ff. 42a–48b, entry B48.

the three collections, which are the entire teachings of the Buddha. They are the single crossroads where all the 84,000 massive stores of the Dharma intersect,[22] they are the one single way by which each and every victorious Buddha has traveled, or travels now, or ever again will travel. As the shorter *Gem of Fine Qualities* says it,

> It is this perfection, nothing else,
> Which is the path that's shared
> By all the Victors, stay they in
> The past, the present, or the future.[23]

People like you and I can go to great Lamas all we want, and receive from them high initiations, or special oral transmissions, and teachings on texts or the like. We can claim to have studied the five great classics,[24] and plumbed

---

[22] *Massive stores of the Dharma:* By tradition the Buddha taught 84,000 huge collections of scripture, one collection for each of the different variants of our negative emotions and harmful habits. There are a number of different positions on the exact quantity of the teachings contained in each of these collections; the view of the greater way is that each such collection consists of the number of pages one could write with the amount of ink that the great mythical elephant named Firmest could carry on his back. See the First Dalai Lama's commentary to the *Treasure House of Higher Knowledge*, f. 26b, entry B11.

[23] *This perfection, nothing else:* The verse is found in the *Shorter Sutra* on the Perfection of Wisdom, entry S30, f. 206a. It is generally considered the ultimate origin of the expression "Steps of the path," and is quoted by Je Tsongkapa in his *Greater Steps*, as well as in Pabongka Rinpoche's own masterpiece on the Steps, and commentary to the *Three Principal Paths*. See respectively f. 10b, entry B26; f. 334b, entry B48; and f. 8b, entry B47 (p. 49 in the English version, entry E9).

[24] *The five great classics:* These are the five great books of early Indian Buddhism studied and debated in major Tibetan monasteries even in Je Tsongkapa's time. As mentioned throughout his *Great Biography*, they are the *Jewel of Realizations* brought from Loving One by Master Asanga (350AD); *Entering the Middle Way*, by Master Chandrakirti (650AD); *Treasure House of Higher Knowledge*, by Master Vasubandhu (335AD); *Abbreviation of Vowed Morality*, by Master Gunaprabha (500AD); and *Commentary on Accurate Perception*, by Master Dharmakirti (650AD). Refer to the *Biography* at p. 143, entry B62; for the five themselves, see respectively entries S23, S9, S26, S7, and S15.

them to their depths, it doesn't matter. But if in the end we are unable to put these Steps into practice within our own lives, joining them all into one, then there's a risk that we'll turn out the way the Great Fifth described it:

> True we see fools
> Who know no better,
> Doing what's wrong
> For things of this life.
>
> But we err worse
> Who've studied much
> The holiest of words,
>
> And yet still see
> Our ultimate hopes
> Swept away on the wind.[25]

So you must turn your learning within, into Dharma: you must take those four great qualities of the Steps to Buddhahood and apply them to your own heart.

And there is more you should know; verses like those of the Master Translator of Taktsang:

> I sing your praises,
> Vast treasure house
> Of fine explanation
> We lacked before,
>
> Elucidation of all
> The highest of speech,
> Especially the diamond way,

---

[25] *Swept away on the wind:* See f. 35a of *The Word of Gentle Voice* (entry B21). The "Great Fifth," as mentioned above in footnote 18 (*You will only lose yourself,* page 35), refers to His Holiness the Fifth Dalai Lama.

> Teachings on all
> The secret groups,
> Especially the Unsurpassed;
>
> On all the parts
> Of both the levels,
> Especially the magic body.[26]

There are as well the words of the Karmapa, Mikyu Dorje, who in the later part of his life developed for Lord Tsongkapa an extraordinary level of admiration, a kind that is found among those of high intelligence, who follow the Dharma not out of faith, but rather out of reason. The lines read in part:

> I make this praise
> To the tradition of
> The Mount of the Heaven of Bliss;
>
> To Tsongkapa,
> For in these days
> When the vast majority
> Of those in our Northern Land
>
> Act only wrong
> With the teachings of the Victors,
> He instead has wiped
> And cleaned away the dirt on them,

---

[26] *Especially the magic body:* The Master Translator of Taktsang, Sherab Rinchen (1405–1477), was one of the foremost scholars of the Sakya tradition of Tibetan Buddhism. The quotation is found on f. 2b of his eulogy to Je Tsongkapa, at entry B75. The lines appear as well in Pabongka Rinpoche's *Gift of Liberation,* and in the famed *Survey of the Schools of Philosophy* by Tuken Lobsang Chukyi Nyima (1737–1802). See f. 301a, entry B48, and f. 35a of entry B59.

The lines beginning from "diamond way" refer to the secret teachings of Buddhism.

Ever faultlessly.[27]

That highest of Victors, Kelsang Gyatso, has said too:

> It is a pure tradition,
> The lineage of the Heaven of Bliss;
> It is no biased
> Or limited school of thought.
>
> It is the essential nectar,
> To learn and practice the Teaching
> So all the open and secret Word
> Seems personal instruction.[28]

And that's just the way it is: our scriptural tradition, that of the Mount of the Heaven of Bliss, is one that is totally complete and spotless, on both sides—in the open and the secret Word. It is a kind of teaching that is found nowhere else. And it possesses a multitude of unique and unrivalled qualities: its depth, the speed with which it works, and so on. Thus it is that this teaching on the Steps of the Path to Buddhahood, as it was inaugurated by the Gentle Protector, Tsongkapa, looks to contain a nearly limitless number of spiritual advices found in none of the other schools, nor even among the older Keepers of the Word.[29]

---

[27] *Ever faultlessly*: Mikyu Dorje (1507–1554) was the Eighth Karmapa, spiritual head of the Karma Kagyu lineage of Tibetan Buddhism, and wrote on a wide range of topics. His verse in praise of Je Tsongkapa is found on ff. 4b–5a of entry B66.

[28] *It is a pure tradition*: Gyalwang Kelsang Gyatso (1708–1757) was the Seventh of the Dalai Lamas. The lines quoted here appear among a group of verses, for developing the Good Heart, found in his collected works (see f. 40a, entry B6).

[29] *The older Keepers of the Word*: Refers to the Kadampas, an inspired group of scholars and meditators from the early days of Buddhism in Tibet, dating from the 11th century. Their name literally means "those for whom every single letter of the teachings (*ka*) turns to instructions (*dampa*) immediately relevant to personal practice." The followers of the tradition of Tsongkapa—

41

Could any system be more profound or far-reaching than this Dharma, the Steps of the Path? Certainly not those teachings that others claim are oh-so-deep, or oh-so-high and inscrutable. People chatter about attaining some realization, some supposed zenith of some very secret way: they talk of termination; they talk about the levels of creation & completion; about the channels and winds and drops; the great seal, or the great completion, whatever.[30] But if one never makes use of these very Steps, they can never even plant the seeds, much less bring the path in full to grow within their mind.

This then is why it is so very important to go through the Steps, in the three stages of learning, and contemplating, and meditating upon them. So it is too that I shall now present you, said our Lama, with just a very brief explanation and oral transmission of the work known as the *Source of All My Good,* for it contains within it the complete heart of the Steps of the Path to Buddhahood.

---

the *Gelukpa* or Way of Virtue, lineage of the Heaven of Bliss—are sometimes called the "later Keepers of the Word." See Pabongka Rinpoche's *Gift of Liberation,* entry B48, ff. 45b-46a.

[30] *The great completion:* This and the other practices mentioned are all details of the secret teachings of Buddhism.

II. How to Take a Lama

The text of the *Source of All My Good* may be divided into four different parts:

> 1) the very root of the path, which is how to take a Lama and serve her or him properly;
>
> 2) how to train your mind, once you have taken a Lama;
>
> 3) a request so that you can attain all the favorable conditions for succeeding in the path, and stop all the circumstances that might prevent you from doing so; and then finally
>
> 4) a prayer that in all your future lives you may be taken under the care of a Lama, and so gain the strength to reach the final end of the various levels and paths.

The first of these is presented in a single verse, the first one of the work—

(1)

The source of all my good
Is my kind Lama, my Lord;

Bless me first to see
That taking myself
To her, or to him,
In the proper way

Is the very root
Of the path, and grant me then
To serve and follow them
With all my strength and reverence.

This Step of taking a Lama is itself divided into two sections: developing clear faith in him or her, which is the very root of the Path; and then building up reverence for them, by considering the great kindness they have paid us. The instruction in developing faith comes in two stages: how to follow a Lama in one's thoughts, and then how to follow them in one's actions.

Now the *Secret Teaching of Sambhuta* says,

You will never be able to take a boat
To the other side of the river
Without a guide who holds the tiller.

You will never reach the end of suffering life
Without a Lama,
Even if you perfect yourself
In every other respect.[31]

---

[31] *Perfect yourself:* The lines do not appear to be in the secret teachings of *Samputa*, despite the similarity of the title. For the latter see entry S35. We do however see them quoted in two commentaries to secret texts found in the Tengyur collection of scripture; see f. 51a of entry S6; and f. 98b of entry S14. Several Tibetan commentators attribute the lines to the famed sutra named

The *Shorter Sutra on the Perfection of Wisdom* concurs:

> The Victorious Buddhas,
> Who possess the highest
> Of all good qualities,
> Speak as one when They say:
>
> "Every single part of the Buddhist way
> Depends on a Spiritual Guide."[32]

It says as well:

> And so the wise
> Who seek the high state of enlightenment
> With a fierce wish deep inside
> Should smash all pride within them,
>
> And like a mass of sick men
> Who flock to medicine for a cure,
> Take themselves to a spiritual guide
> And serve them single-mindedly.[33]

Our Gentle Savior, Tsongkapa the Great, has too spoken these words:

> There is a single key
> For finding a perfect start to reach
> Your every wish, both happiness
> In the short run and ultimately;

House of the Jewel Trees (*Ganda Vyuha*); and we do see there this same metaphor, although not in the same versed form; see for example ff. 231a, 251a, and 259b of entry S28.

[32] *Depends on a spiritual guide:* These words of the Buddha himself are found on f. 200a of entry S30.

[33] *Serve them, single-mindedly:* See again entry S30, this time at ff. 205b–206a.

> And the highest words ever spoken
> Speak it always the same:
> It is your Lama.
>
> And so you must devote yourself
> To meditation upon her, or him,
> Upon the essence of all
> The three different kinds of refuge;
> Ask them, for all your goals.[34]

All these lines are saying the same thing: If you have any hope of reaching up to the high spiritual qualities of the various levels and paths, then from the outset you must absolutely find and follow a Lama who can show you how to do so.

And the Lama that we are describing here is not just any one you might happen to come across; it's not just anyone they call a "Lama." Rather, he or she must have in them the ten high qualities described in the *Jewel of the Sutras.* They must first of all be subdued, at peace, and at high peace; that is to say, they must possess all three of the trainings.[35] They must display fine spiritual qualities that exceed those of their student, and exhibit exceptional effort. They should have a total mastery of the Dharma in the form of scripture, and should have realized suchness. They should be highly skilled in teaching the Dharma; they must have a great love

---

[34] *Ask them, for all your goals:* The lines are found in a letter of advice from Je Tsongkapa to one Yunten Gyatso of the district of Tulung, Tibet. See f. 208a, entry B27.

[35] *All three of the trainings:* These are the exceptional trainings of morality, concentration, and wisdom. The original quotation from the *Jewel* of Maitreya is found on ff. 20a–20b of entry S25. The importance of the qualifications of the Lama is indicated by the fact that the same words are quoted in works like the *Greater Steps* of Je Tsongkapa; the First Panchen Lama's *Path to Bliss;* Pabongka Rinpoche's own *Gift of Liberation,* and his commentary to the *Three Principal Paths.* See respectively f. 23a of entry B26; f. 9a of entry B57; f. 134b of entry B48; and f. 6a of entry B47 (p. 41 of the English translation, entry E9).

for their disciples; and they must never become tired or discouraged in their teaching, no matter how much or how often they are called upon to do so.

We are though now in the days of degeneration, and so perhaps it is difficult to find someone who possesses each and every one of these qualifications. In such a case, we must follow the advice of the Lord of Lamas:

> If you take my advice,
> Man of the land of Gyalkam,
> Take yourself to the ultimate
> Spiritual guide:
>
> To one who grasps Reality,
> To one who has controlled their senses,
> Who takes your heart away
> As soon as you lay your eyes on them;
>
> To the one that,
> When you follow what they teach,
> The good in you begins to flower,
> And the bad begins to fade.[36]

These and other such lines are telling us that the Lama we seek must at least possess a complete set of five different qualities: they must have brought their mind under control, by following the three trainings; they must have realized thusness; and they must have love.

As a bare minimum, the Lama must surely fit the following description. He or she must occupy themselves more with

---

[36] *The good begins to flower:* The lines are found in an extraordinary letter of advice written by Je Tsongkapa to himself (he hails from the area of Gyalkam), where he poses numbered questions, and then answers them in the form of profound instruction. It is interesting to note that this is the final work in a large collection of shorter pieces by the Master; the first title is the *Mountain of Blessings* itself, which brings us full circle. See f. 271b, entry B36.

the Dharma than with the things of the world. They must as well occupy themselves more with the concerns of the future life, than with those of the present one. They must occupy themselves more with helping others, than with helping themselves. She or he is never careless in what they do, or say, or think. And, finally, they never lead their disciples along a path which is mistaken.

Suppose you are able to find a Lama like the one we have described above. What are the benefits you can expect from following them properly? Simply put, you will win each and every good thing in this and all your future lives. What are the dangers of refusing to follow them, or of following them less than properly? You will undergo a great mass of unendurable pain, in both the short term and the long. You must seek to grasp these facts fully.

Your *Lama is* like *the source,* he or she is like the very root, from which *every single good* quality of all the different levels and paths of both the open and secret teachings spring. If you ever succeed in stopping a single personal fault, it will be because of them. If you ever manage to cultivate a single spiritual quality, any good at all, that too will come from them. The whole range of virtues, from the final attainment of secret Union on down to having a single wholesome thought, all flow from them.

Your Lama is also the one and only "source" in the sense of being the embodiment or actuality of all the mighty deeds, all the great good, that all the victorious Buddhas perform in their holy actions, words, and thoughts. Try now to develop this root of the path—clear faith in him or her.

If with eyes made clear by this faith you begin to see your Lama as a real Buddha, then the blessing of a real Buddha will follow in your mind-stream. It's essential therefore that you train your mind in the relevant parts described in the texts on the Steps: the reasons why you should see that your Lama is a Buddha; the reasons why you can see that your Lama is a Buddha; how to see them, and so on.

The word *"kind"* in the verse here is meant to convey the Step of building up reverence for your Lama by considering all the kind things they have done for you. The word *"Lord"* is a translation of the Sanskrit word *Svami*, a word that applies to someone who is like a crowning jewel which all the beings of the universe, including the great worldly beings of power, humbly place above their heads.

What does it mean to *"follow* your Lama properly?" You must understand that it means to surrender yourself completely to him or her. Here you should take yourself to them in the way of an obedient child, and with the rest of the nine attitudes described in the *House of the Jewel Trees*.[37]

---

[37] *The nine attitudes:* The nine are mentioned in Je Tsongkapa's *Greater Steps* at f. 27b, entry B26, and are listed fully in the First Panchen Lama's *Path of Ease* (f. 10b, entry B57). The original sutra subsumes two volumes of the canon and as briefly noted before includes repeated, exquisite descriptions of these and similar attitudes to develop towards one's Lama. See especially the second volume, ff. 229b–230a, and the entire section from ff. 225 to 250, entry S28.

The nine attitudes taught in the sutra are as follows:

1) Like an obedient child, give up your own will and submit yourself to your Lama.

2) Like a diamond, be solid in your devotion to him or her, and let no relative or friend come between you.

3) Like the earth itself, accept any task your Lama may load upon you.

4) Like the great mountains at the edge of the world, stay unshakable in your service, regardless of any troubles that come.

5) Like a hand servant, carry out any task she or he gives you, never seeking to avoid it, no matter how distasteful it may seem.

6) Like the dust of the earth, seek the lowest position, giving up all pride, all pretension, all conceit.

7) Like a sturdy vehicle, undertake any burden your Lama may give you, however heavy.

8) Like a loyal dog, stay without anger, regardless of how your Lama might berate or scold you.

9) No matter how much you have to go here and there in the service of your Lama, be willing to go, like a boat that never complains.

To put it briefly, you must absolutely conduct yourself *properly* in this regard; you must follow precisely every one of the classical descriptions of how to find and follow a Lama. If the cornerstone of a house—the walls of its foundation— are solid, then the house itself is solid. If the *roots* of a tree are planted firmly in the soil, then the branches and fruit and all the rest grow strong.

What we hope to grow is the path, in its entirety: all the Steps from recognizing the importance of the spiritual leisure and fortune of our present circumstances, on up to the attainment of secret Union itself. We must find sure and solid knowledge, we must see, that taking ourselves to our Lama properly will bring all of this about without any difficulty at all.

The entire subject of how to follow your Lama in your thoughts is revealed in the words "first to see." Thus you must come to see your spiritual Friend as a real Buddha; and this brings us to how you should follow them in your actions.

How can we please our Lama? Relative to the path which is shared, you should use the instructions found in the discussions on how to find and follow a Lama in general. Relative to the way of the secret Word, use the instructions in the *Fifty Verses on Lamas*.[38] Both of these describe how you should, to the very best of your ability, *"with all your strength,"* gladly take up any difficult task in any of the three doors of expression—of body, speech, or mind—in order to please him or her.

There are different levels of how we pay homage to our Lama: to offer him or her gifts, material things; to give ourselves up to their service, their honor; and to take what they have taught us and put it into actual practice, accomplishing our spiritual goals. Each of these is higher

---

[38] *Fifty Verses on Lamas:* A classic description of Lama devotion written by the Indian Buddhist master Ashvagosha, circa 100AD. See entry S4.

than the one before it, and the last one is supreme.

The root text here then is saying that we must take ourselves to our Lama in a whole different number of ways, in keeping with our personal mental capacity.

And as you *serve* your Lama, remember. When a farmer goes to plant his or her seeds, whatever work they do in the field they do for their own sake. It's not as if they are doing the field a favor. Here I am the same. It's me who hopes to reach freedom from pain, and the state of knowing all things. To do so, I must take up certain things and give up others; but I am like a person who is blind—I am totally ignorant of which of these things are which.

My spiritual Friend is here to lead the blind; and in my service of him or her I am obliged to do anything required of me, no matter how exhausting, no matter how distasteful— so long as nothing morally wrong is involved.

And I am not to view this service as if I were laboring for someone else; on the contrary, I should not even see it as a burden, but rather as a reward: it is my great good fortune to have the opportunity. And so I must succeed in serving her or him in both my thoughts and actions, with the deepest feelings of *reverence*.

If our service of our Lama is good, then in all our future lives we will find ourselves taken under the care of Lamas. Then too we can count the life we have found now as the first in a long and unbroken series of lives in which we enjoy each of the eight spiritual leisures, and the ten fortunes. And there will never again be any mistake in this particular arithmetic: we will always enjoy the exact number of circumstances needed to follow our practice of the Dharma, and so finally reach the state of perfect enlightenment.

The words *"bless me"* here mean "embellish me"; which is to say, "transform the condition of my mind." A minute ago my mind was twisted wrong, and joined with every kind of bad thought. Now, in the very next moment, may I be blessed with the good fortune of being able to find and follow my Lama properly, with every reverence; may my mind be straightened, and become filled with each and every Step of the path. This is the thing I ask, my Lama.

The explanation of the words "bless me" here applies as well to each of the other verses in which they appear.

III. Advice to Take
the Essence of Life

This brings us to the second major part of the text itself, which describes how to train the mind, once you have properly taken a Lama. This part comes in two Steps: urgent advice to take the essence of the present life, with its spiritual leisure and fortune; and a description of just how to take this essence. The first step is contained in the single verse that follows next:

(2)

Bless me first to realize
That the excellent life
Of leisure I've found
Just this once

Is ever so hard to find
And ever so valuable;

Grant me then
To wish, and never stop to wish,
That I could take
Its essence night and day.

The phrase about finding a life like this *"just this once"* is meant to indicate that we would never be able to find this kind of life on a regular basis in the future.

You may wonder too why, at a point where the concepts of spiritual leisure and fortune are being presented, the verse says only *"life of leisure,"* and not "life of leisure and fortune." The point is that we actually do possess the entire set of eight spiritual leisures, which consist of being free of the eight ways that a person can lack opportunity. These lacks of opportunity are birth in the three lower realms,[39] or as a long-life being of pleasure; as a barbarian; as a person with a mistaken worldview; as someone who is handicapped; or in a period of history when the victorious Buddha has yet to appear in the world.

We do have all five of the spiritual fortunes that relate to one's self, as described in the following verse:

> Born as a human,
> In a central land,
> And having one's faculties
> All complete;
> Not lost to the last of karma,
> And feeling faith for the place.[40]

Here "born in a central land" refers to a land where there exists the "core of the Dharma," meaning that there are people in the country who keep the vows of the "four

---

[39] *Three lower realms:* According to Buddhism there are six different types of rebirth. These are birth as a hell-being, a craving spirit, an animal, a human, one who is nearly a full pleasure being, and a full pleasure being. The first three types of birth are known as the three lower realms.

Pleasure beings enjoy extremely long lives in a temporary paradise, and then normally fall to hell after exhausting their good karma. The classic presentation of the six rebirths is found in the third chapter of the *Treasure House of Higher Knowledge,* by the 4th-century Buddhist philosopher Vasubandhu; a typical commentary would be that of the First Dalai Lama, Gyalwa Gendun Drup (1391–1474). See entry S26, ff. 7a–10b, and entry B11, ff. 73b–108a.

[40] *Born as a human:* The classic source for the description of spiritual fortunes is the *Levels of Listeners,* one of the major divisions of the *Levels of Practitioners,* written by the Indian Buddhist sage Asanga in the 4th century. The prose origin for the verse found here is located on ff. 3b–4a of the work, at entry S5.

attendants to the Buddha." This refers to the full ordinations for a man and a woman, along with the novice ordinations for the same. The main component of the core is the fully ordained monk.

"Not lost to the last of karma" means not having collected, and then failed to clear from oneself, the karma that comes from committing one of the "immediate," heinous bad deeds.[41]

The place from where each and every pure and good thing grows is the teaching on discipline; here the word "discipline" can by extension be applied to the entire contents of the canon—the three collections of scripture—since they all function to discipline one's mind.[42] We do then possess the fortune of having faith in the holy books.

Let us examine though whether we have the five fortunes that relate to what is outside ourselves. The classic reference here is:

> The Buddha is come,
> And taught the holy Dharma.
> The teaching remains,

---

[41] *Immediate bad deeds:* Buddhism teaches that there are five misdeeds which are so evil that they are sure to lead one to a hell birth in the very next life. The deeds are, from most serious to least, the following: causing a schism in the community of monks; attempting to kill a Buddha; killing someone who has reached nirvana; killing one's mother, and killing one's father. A full discussion of the five is found in the fourth chapter of Master Vasubandhu's *Treasure House of Higher Knowledge,* and in commentaries such as the one by Jampay Yang of Chim (c. 1280). See entry S26, ff. 14b–15a, and entry B22, ff. 240b–246a.

[42] *Discipline one's mind:* The collection on discipline, or vowed morality, is actually only one of the three sections of the original Buddhist canon; the point is that all the scriptures though teach the absolute importance of moral behavior. For a description of the three collections see footnote 20 (*A gold and jewel rosary,* page 36).

As do the ones who follow.
There is compassion
For the sake of others.[43]

Here the Buddha must have come and still be present in the world. He or his direct disciples must be teaching the Dharma. The resulting teachings must also remain, and this during the period before his final passing beyond all sorrow. Certain of his disciples must observe other disciples actually achieve the four results,[44] after he has taught them; and these disciples must undertake to follow the same practices too.

All four of the fortunes just explained have been possessed even by the likes of the monk Udayi,[45] whereas the same cannot be said even for the Savior Nagarjuna, who lacked them in their literal form. We too have met our Lamas, who are no different from a Buddha, and they have spoken the Dharma and so on; these are a full substitute yes, but we cannot say that we have all those fortunes in their literal form. We do however enjoy all eight of the spiritual leisures; these then are our primary advantage, and it's with this fact in mind that the verse reads "life of leisure."

---

[43] *For the sake of others:* Again the original source in prose is Master Asanga's *Levels of Listeners.* See ff. 4b–5a, entry S5.

[44] *The four results:* The four fruits of the "way of virtue," which in this case refers to the direct perception of selflessness. The four are to attain the state of a foe destroyer; of one who need never again take rebirth in this realm of desire; of one who must take one more rebirth in this realm; and of one who has "entered the stream"—one who, due to their realization of selflessness, is clearly headed for freedom. The four are presented for example in the second and sixth chapters of Master Vasubandhu's *Treasure House,* with its commentary by the First Dalai Lama. See entry S26, ff. 4b, 20b; and entry B11, ff. 48b–50a, 175b–176a.

[45] *Even by the likes of the monk Udayi:* The monk was one of the members of the Buddha's inner circle, but committed a series of misdeeds which actually led to the creation of a number of the rules for monks. See Professor Edgerton's *Buddhist Hybrid Sanskrit Dictionary,* entry E3, pp. 128–129, as well as the First Dalai Lama and Jampay Yang of Chim—f. 10a, entry B11, and f. 11b, entry B22, respectively. This same concept of Udayi possessing spiritual fortunes that we lack is found as well in Pabongka Rinpoche's *Gift,* f. 157b, entry B48.

What does it mean when the reference says, "There is compassion for the sake of others?" The "others" here refers to ourselves; our sponsors and Lamas and other such persons act for our sake, motivated by compassion, to see that we are provided with all the conditions that will facilitate our practice of the Dharma: they give us food, or clothes, and other necessities; they teach us the Dharma; and so on. Therefore this phrase should be understood as describing the good fortune to have around us those who give us the things we need to practice.

So you and I are free of the eight ways in which a person can lack spiritual opportunity; and yet we fail to work here now, in the days when we do have a Dharma to practice. We find ourselves locked in the handcuffs of the present life; we throw ourselves into all sorts of meaningless activities aimed at gaining material things, or other people's approval, or a taste of fame; we want to fit into the world's way of life, and so on. These make us so busy that it's almost as if we have taken special care to invent a ninth way of lacking spiritual opportunity.

We have here a wonderful life and body of exactly the same kind that holy persons in the past have used to achieve enlightenment itself; we though use these things as a big pot in which to stock up our bad deeds. We have turned our spiritual leisure and fortune into a rich opportunity to suffer.

In order not to lose the good qualities of this life in our future lives, we must manage to take some special essence of the circumstances we have found, just this once; we must use this lifetime where everything has come together, where there is not a single piece of the whole incomplete. If we fail in this endeavor, then it will be extremely difficult for us to find a life of spiritual leisure and fortune ever again.

Whether you will be able to gain such a life again or not you must judge from looking within yourself, to see if all the causes of winning the various leisures and fortunes are there, or not. It's no use to look outside, to see whether or not there are a lot of human beings around. Humans are one of the six forms of suffering life, and until all six disappear you will see no end to humans. There will always be some good number around, but if they lack this complement of leisure and fortune, a big population will only mean an even more tremendous amassing of sins. You should take no comfort, said our Lama, in the fact that there is such an abundant supply of raw material for the circle of suffering life.

"Well then," you may ask, "just what is it that causes the leisures and fortunes to come about?" Attaining the good life, one of spiritual leisure, begins with morals kept very well. This morality must be joined with giving and the other five perfections; and the glue that holds it all together is to make the very purest of prayers. Therefore *finding* a life like ours is first of all something difficult because of the causes needed to bring it about.

People like you and I are forever committing non-virtuous deeds, and this is the single greatest obstacle to our reaching the state of spiritual leisure and fortune ever again. Beyond this are statements from the *Foundation Word on Vowed Morality,* and other texts, which describe how those born as animals are fewer than those born in one of the other births of misery; those born as humans are fewer than the animals; and even among humans, those born in a country where the Buddha's teachings have spread are fewer still.[46]

---

[46] *Fewer still:* The *Foundation Word on Vowed Morality* is one of the four famed explanatory sutras on the subject of vowed morality. An exquisite passage found there begins as follows:

> And then Lord Buddha touched the very tip of his precious fingernail to the ground, and raised it up, and showed it to the assembled monks. He said,

> Monks! Which do you think are more: the atoms of dust here on the tip of my fingernail, or the atoms of dust contained in the entire planet of earth?

To be born in such a land, and then go on to actually encounter the Dharma with a mind and body so very special as the one which we now possess, is an occurrence which borders on the impossible. This shows how a life like ours is difficult to find by its very nature as well.

There is yet a third way to show how difficult it is to find a life so opportune as our own. This involves using a metaphor, such as the following from the *Letter to a Friend:*

And the monks replied,

> Oh Reverend One, Oh Conqueror, the atoms of dust there on the tip of Your precious fingernail are less, they are certainly less, they are most certainly less, they are infinitely less. If one compared them to the number of atoms of dust in this great orb they would not amount to a hundredth, nor even a thousandth, nor a hundred thousandth, nor any fraction at all, nor any part—no countable part, no comparison, no basis for a comparison.

The Conqueror spoke again:

> Monks! Think of the number of atoms of dust in the entire planet: this stands for the number of beings who are in hell now and who—after they die—will migrate back to hell. Now think of the number of atoms of dust on my fingernail: this stands for the number of beings who are in hell now and who—after they die—will migrate to the world of humans.

The Buddha continues his description in a similar vein for all the other types of rebirths—including humans who are reborn as hell beings (as many as atoms of dust in the planet), as opposed to humans who are reborn as humans (as many as the atoms of dust on his fingernail).

This presentation appears throughout the various books on the Steps to Buddhahood: see those of Je Tsongkapa, Pabongka Rinpoche, and the First Panchen Lama (entry B26, f. 81a; entry B48, f. 163b; and entry B57, ff. 30a–30b, respectively).

Suppose a turtle in the sea were to rise
And poke his head right through the hole
Of a wooden ring as it drifted around
The surface of the great salt sea.

The odds of being born a human
As opposed to birth as an animal
Are even more remote; make it come,
Lord of Humankind, by living holy Dharma.[47]

Right now we have the time to practice religion. We possess the outer condition we need to succeed, for we have come into contact with a Lama, a spiritual Friend who is just like Lord Buddha himself. We also enjoy the inner condition, since our minds are not defective in any way, and we are endowed with the intelligence required to advance through the stages of learning, contemplation, and meditation.

If I truly undertake to do so, it is certain that I can achieve everything from temporal goals, such as achieving a good and useful kind of birth in the higher forms of life—among humans or the beings of pleasure—on up to the ultimate goal of becoming the Keeper of the Diamond themselves.[48]

All this can be achieved because of the extraordinary kind of life I have now gained; seek to understand this fact, try to truly recognize how significant the one chance is.

Certain signs will come if you succeed in making yourself aware of your spiritual leisure and fortune. Think of a person who is completely engrossed, either in some great good luck, or in some great misfortune. Every time they wake up at night, these thoughts of happiness or unhappiness well up in them, vivid and automatic.

---

[47] *A turtle in the sea:* These well-known lines are found in a letter from the realized being Nagarjuna (c. 200AD) to his friend, King Udayibhadra. See f. 43b, entry S19, as well as p. 92 of the English translation, entry E8.

[48] *Keeper of the Diamond themselves:* That is, Buddhahood in the Diamond Way: enlightenment in one lifetime.

What we are requesting from our Lama here is that they bless us to achieve this same level of obsession: *Bless me first to realize that the excellent life I've found,* complete with every spiritual *leisure, is hard to find and*—once found—is *ever so valuable.*

Now, in the one and only time I have ever managed to win this diamond body and life, let me think of how the circle of suffering has absolutely no beginning; how one must normally practice for many millions of years to reach the state of a Buddha; and other such truths. *And grant me then to wish, and never stop to wish, that I could take this life's essence night and day:* that I could at every given moment keep this precious time from being lost to actions which are pointless, devoid of any meaning.

Steps Shared with Those
of Lesser Capacity

IV. Steps Shared with Those of Lesser Capacity

This brings us to our description of how actually to take the essence of this life. This part itself has three; the first is how to train one's mind in the Steps of the path which are shared with persons of lesser spiritual capacity, and is covered in the next two verses of the root text:

(3,4)

My body and the life in it
Are fleeting as the bubbles
In the sea froth of a wave.

Bless me first thus to recall
The death that will destroy me soon;
And help me find sure knowledge
That after I have died

The things I've done, the white or black,
And what these deeds will bring to me,
Follow always close behind,
As certain as my shadow.

Grant me then
Ever to be careful,
To stop the slightest
Wrongs of many wrongs we do,

And try to carry out instead
Each and every good
Of the many that we may.

And so we have attained this very special kind of life, with its spiritual leisure and fortune. But *my body and the life in it are fleeting*, forever changing, and every passing moment they move inexorably closer to my death.

But that's not all—there are conditions all around me that can strike and kill me in an instant: things like illness and harmful spirits, sudden disasters, attacks upon me by the very four elements that make up my own body. They stand around me ready to snatch away my life, like a pack of dogs circling around a piece of fresh meat, lusting after it.[49]

Still more, my body is like a *bubble in the sea froth of a wave*; it has no power to resist even some very minor harm: we can see with our own two eyes that even the prick of a thorn can lead to a person's death.

In sum, my body and life are fragile; so *death will destroy me soon*. Here you should use the instructions on your coming death that we find in works like the longer and briefer presentations of the Steps of the path by our Lord, Tsongkapa. These sections cover the three principles of death and the nine reasons for them, along with the three resolutions to be made.[50]

---

[49] *Like a pack of dogs circling:* The Tibetan original at this point actually refers to "dogs who circle the talisman." In certain cases of illness brought on by harmful spirits, a Lama will by tradition come to the house of the patient and prepare a small likeness or talisman representing the person. A ritual is held centered around the talisman to help remove the evil influence. The figurine is fashioned from a soft dough and, at the end of the ceremony, is carried outside and placed on the ground—where hungry Tibetan mastiffs are usually waiting to gulp it down. The image here then is of a pack of dogs crowded eagerly around the ritual attendant as they carry out the prize.

[50] *The three principles of death:* This presentation of death appears in many of the texts on the Steps to Buddhahood, and is summarized as follows in a note from the English translation of Je Tsongkapa's *Principal Teachings of Buddhism* (the text of his *Three Principal Paths*).

In his masterwork *A Gift of Liberation,* Pabongka Rinpoche lists six benefits of keeping your mind on death: your practice becomes really pure; it gains power; the thoughts help you start practice; they help you strive hard during your practice; they help bring your practice to a successful conclusion; and in the hour of death you go with satisfaction, for you know you have spent your life meaningfully.

The Rinpoche also lists six problems that come from not keeping your mind on death: you neglect your religious life, and spend all your days in thoughts of what to eat or wear—this life's distractions; you consider death occasionally but always think it will come later, and delay your practice; or you do practice, but for the wrong reason—with hopes of reputation; you practice but with no enthusiasm, and drop it after a while; you get deeper into this life, your attitude gets worse, and life begins to hurt you; and at death you naturally feel intense regret, for you have wasted all your efforts on this present life.

The three principles, for how actually to keep your mind on death, have three reasons each, making a total of nine. First of all, death is certain: no power in the universe can stop death when it arrives; there is no way to add time to your life, you come closer to death every minute; and even while you are alive, the free time available for your practice is extremely limited before you have to die.

The second principle is that there is absolutely no certainty when you will die. We are in a time and realm where the length of life is uncertain; we can be sure we will never have enough time to defeat all our enemies, raise up all our friends, and still complete our religious practice before we die. The things that can kill us are many; the things that keep us alive are few. And in general the body we have is fragile, weak: a small splinter in the hand can give us an infection that kills us—we are like bubbles, like candles in a windstorm.

The third principle is that, at the moment of death, nothing at all can help us but our spiritual practice. None of your money or things can help you. None of your friends or family can help you—they can be holding you tightly by the arms and legs, but still you slip away alone. And not even your own body can help you—you have to give up your most cherished possession, your beloved body, along with everything else.

The three principles call for three resolves on our part. Knowing that we shall have to die, we must resolve to begin our practice. Knowing that we could die any time, we must quit our worldly work immediately and start our practice today. And finally, since nothing else can help us, we must devote ourselves to our practice only. A man who is hiking many miles doesn't fill up his pack with a lot of junk that he won't be needing.

The above points are paraphrased from the works on the Steps of the path by Lord Tsongkapa (entry B26, ff. 65–75) and Pabongka Rinpoche (entry B48, ff. 168–182). For the last point mentioned in the text, the meditation on what it's like to die, we quote the Rinpoche directly (ff. 182b–183a):

They show how our death is certain, and how uncertain

They try all different kinds of treatments and holy rituals but your condition gets worse and worse. The doctors start lying to you. Your friends and relatives say all sorts of cheery things to your face, but behind your back they start wrapping up your affairs, because everyone can see you're going to die. Your body starts to lose its familiar warmth. It's hard to breathe. The nostrils collapse. The lips curl back. The color starts to drain from your face. All sorts of repulsive signs begin to show, inside and outside of you.

You think of all the wrong things you did in your life, and wish so badly you had never done them. You can't quite be sure if you ever really got rid of them all when you confessed; or that you really did any true good deed.

Then comes the final pain, the unspeakable searing pain that comes with death. The basic building blocks of your body begin their domino collapse, you are blinded by catastrophic images, hallucinations of pure terror crowd into your mind, and carry you away, and the whole world you have been living blinks out.

People take your corpse and wrap it up in a sheet and lay it in some corner. They hang up a curtain to hide it. Somebody lights up a smudgy little candle and leaves it there. If you're one of those reincarnated lamas, they dress you up in your fancy ritual robes and try to make you look good.

Right now we are all running around trying to arrange ourselves a nice house, soft clothes, cozy chairs. But you know the custom here in Tibet—when you die they'll tie your arms and legs up against your chest with a leather strap, carry the body far from town, and throw it naked out on the rocks.

Right now we all go home and try to cook ourselves up some delectable dish—but there will come a day when you stand there praying for a little taste of those cakes they offer the spirits of the dead. Right now we have the big name—they call us Doctor Professor, or Respected Sir, or Your Reverence. But there will come a day when they look at your body and call you nothing but "that stinking corpse." There will come a day when the title they put in front of your name is "the late," or "that guy they used to call..."

So now when you respected lamas out there in the audience look at your ritual robes, let it come into your thoughts that these are the robes they will dress your

we are of when it will come. When it does, none of the people close to us, nor any of the things we own, nor anything else of the kind can help us. In the end, not even our body can be of any assistance.

Think on these points, *recall* them, again and again. The object here is not to reach a point where you sit in some confused terror over the death that's coming to you. Rather you must come to see that, at the moment of death and as you take your future life, only the Dharma can help you: everything else turns useless. Remember the words of the omniscient Buton, who has spoken:

> You are not long in this life—
> Death comes quick;
> You step ever nearer to it
> With every moment that passes,
> Moving on like an animal
> Dragged to the slaughterhouse.
>
> Your plans for today
> Your plans for tomorrow
> Will never all be filled;
> Let go all your thousand plans,
> Devote yourself to one.

---

remains in after you have expired. And all the rest of us, when we look at our bedsheets before we go to sleep, should try to remember that these are what they will wrap our stinking corpse in when we die. As Milarepa said,

> That frightful corpse they talk about
> Is the very body you wear, meditator.

He means look at your own body now, and always see the future corpse.

You will be summoned into
The awesome presence of Lord Death;
The end is lying on your bed,
The breathing stops, the life is gone.

And on this day,
My Rinchen Drup,
Nothing but the Dharma
Is any help to you.[51]

Pa Dampa Sangye too has said:

The results of deeds you've done,
The cause and consequence,
Are finally true and fixed.

People of Dingri listen:
Avoid then any bad deed,
Any wrong at all.[52]

And then he states:

In the land beyond us,
Friends and relatives are few;
People of Dingri listen:
Turn your thoughts to Dharma.[53]

---

[51] *Nothing but the Dharma:* See f. 211a of his famed *History of Buddhism* (entry B53). The advice is to himself, for Master Buton's full name was Rinchen Drup (1290–1364). He was a consummate scholar of both the secret and open teachings, and Je Tsongkapa was much influenced by his writings and by his direct disciples. Buton Rinpoche also played a major role in the organization of the Buddhist canon in its Tibetan translation.

[52] *Avoid then any bad deed:* Pa Dampa Sangye (d. 1117?) was an Indian Buddhist master who helped bring the teachings to Tibet, and in particular began the lineage of a practice called the "Termination of Suffering." The lines here are found in a collection of advices to the Tibetans of an area called Dingri. See f. 3a, entry B43.

[53] *Turn your thoughts to the Dharma:* This passage is from the same work as the preceding; see f. 4a, entry B43.

The master teacher of Bodong, whose name was Jikdrel Chokley Namgyal, has also said:

> The existence of past and future lives can be understood as well through logical reasoning. If the human body could occur without any proper cause, then every existing object might just as well be stuffed full of human bodies. If the human body could occur without any involvement of previous consciousness—if it could come from physical matter alone—then every bit of dirt, every rock, every mountain and stream might just as well be stuffed full of human bodies.
>
> For those who deny that life goes on, hearing these lines is like being struck by a bolt of lightning. There are moreover quite numerous accounts of many wise and accomplished practitioners who have used clairvoyance to perceive the past and future lives, as well as the state between death and rebirth, which they and others have passed through. There are also cases like those of the non-Buddhist adepts who attain clairvoyance that allows them to recall eighty of their different lives.[54]

Since nothing else can help then, it is essential that we give up on life and be sure to devote ourselves to death, by practicing some pure form of the Dharma, as a way to assist our future

---

[54] *Eighty of their different lives:* Original source of quotation not found; we have not yet input this collection. Bodong Rinpoche, full name Bodong Panchen Chokley Namgyal (1375–1450), was one of the most prolific writers in the history of Buddhism—his collected works subsume no less than 137 volumes. See entry B52.

self. It's not as if, *after* you and I *have died*, the stream of our mind just stops and we turn into nothing. Rather we have no choice but to take another birth. And there are no more than two places where we can take that birth: in the higher realms of happiness, or the lower realms of misery.

We have absolutely no control over which of the two places we go; we must follow where we are sent by the separate causes for each place, and these causes are *the things we've done, the white and black,* respectively.

Our mental streams contain very, very few of the causes that will take us to a higher birth; but we have a vast multitude of the causes that will lead us to one of the births of misery. Right now we are doing both white deeds, and black deeds: the good and the bad. At the moment of death, the power of one or the other will be activated, and force us over to our next birth. The seeds of the deeds which are more plentiful are the kind that are likely to be activated.

And after we cross over to our new birth, the fair or foul consequences of our virtue or our evil will *follow close behind*. These consequences can never go wrong; good must come from the good, and bad from the bad. They will attach themselves to my consciousness and pass on to wherever it goes, *as certain as my shadow.*

This fact—that pleasure and pain are the respective results of good and evil—is spoken in the various collections of the immaculate Word of the victorious Buddhas: in the sutras, in the books of discipline, and so on. They describe things like how karma is certain to produce similar results; how it multiplies; how consequences of a karma not committed can never be experienced; and how the consequences of a karma committed can never just fade away on their own. It is spoken as well that:

> The karma of sentient kind
> Never just fades away,
> Even in hundreds

Of millions of years.

When the causes convene
And the time is come,
The consequences
Can do nothing but flower.[55]

Master Bodongwa quotes these same lines from sutra and says,

People like you and I may have blurry eyes
but we must look on this Word of the Buddha
as perfectly accurate. If you die, then die;
if you drop from old age, then drop; but if
nothing else keep your trust in the Teacher.[56]

---

[55] *Never just fades away:* These lines are some of the most famous in all of Buddhist literature. They were spoken by Lord Buddha himself and occur throughout the sutras on vowed morality as a sort of refrain—for example in the *Divisions of Vowed Morality*, and the *Foundation Word*. See entry S33, first volume, ff. 127a, 177a, and 276b; as well as entry S32, first volume, ff. 41a, 44b–45a, 90a–90b, 114b, and so on. Their contents are alluded to also in the famed *Sutra of Cosmic Play*; see entry S31, f. 203a.

The importance of the concept that the power of an act cannot just fade away after we commit it is indicated by the fact that many of the earlier Indian masters include the lines in their philosophical commentaries. Master Nagarjuna (200AD), for example, alludes to them in his *Root Text on Wisdom*, and *Beyond All Fear*. Master Bhavya (490–570AD) speaks of them in his famous *Blaze of Reasoning*, as does Master Avalokitavrata in his *Extensive Commentary to the "Lamp of Wisdom."*

The renowned Chandrakirti (650AD) refers to the quotation in his *Clarification of the Words;* his *Commentary to the "400 Verses";* and his *Commentary to the "Seventy Verses on Emptiness."* It appears as well in Master Parahita's explanation of the same work. See, respectively, entry S16, f. 10a; entry S17, f. 67a; entry S22, f. 184b; entry S3, f. 264a; entry S10, ff. 107a and 126b; entry S8, f. 150b; entry S12, f. 314a; and entry S21, f. 355a.

In Tibet as well the verse and the idea behind it have been considered indispensable, and it is referred to in a great number of works on the Steps of the Path. See for example the treatises of Geshe Drolungpa, Je Tsongkapa, Changkya Ngawang Chunden, and Pabongka Rinpoche himself, at entry B55, ff. 55a–55b; entry B26, f. 106b and 129a; entry B18, f. 78a; and entry B48, f. 230a.

[56] *If nothing else keep your trust:* Original source of quotation not found; it is in a very old local dialect, but the meaning seems correct. For information about the author, see footnote 54 (*Eighty of their different lives*, page 73).

The thinking behind these lines is expressed in a verse by the Master Shantideva:

> The way karma works
> Is beyond comprehension;
> Only the All-Knowing
> Know it.[57]

Because of these facts you and I must seek a way to *find sure knowledge*, where we recognize the truth of the simply limitless workings of karma & consequences described by the Teacher. Once we have found this knowledge, we then understand that the necessary consequence of all the harmful deeds we have amassed up to now will be for us to pass on to the births of misery in our next life.

And what of these three lower realms? Think fiercely on their sufferings: the heat of the molten steel, the cold; the hunger, the thirst, exhaustion and terror; being unable to talk, living in dark ignorance, eating each other to survive, and all the rest. It will bring you fear, and from the depths of your heart you will go for shelter to the ones who can protect you: to the Three Jewels.[58]

If harmful actions provide the causes that push us to

---

[57] *Only the All-Knowing know it:* The lines are found in the fourth chapter of *A Guide to the Bodhisattva's Way of Life,* a famed manual for aspiring saints dating from the 8th century. See f. 8a, entry S36.

[58] *The ones who can protect you:* The three lower realms described here are— respectively—the worlds of hell beings, craving spirits, and animals. The Three Jewels that can protect us from them are the Buddha, Dharma, and Sangha.

The Buddha Jewel is defined as "That ultimate source of protection: the One who has reached the final end of their own goals, and the ability to achieve others' as well."

The Dharma Jewel is "The pure side of existence, either in the form of the end of all suffering, or the path to that end."

The Sangha Jewel, finally, consists of "All those who are realized"—that is, the Community of all people who have realized emptiness directly. For these and an illuminating discussion on the act of taking refuge, see Kedrup Tenpa Dargye, *Analysis of the Perfection of Wisdom,* ff. 41b–52a, Vol. 2, at entry B41.

these lower realms, then needless to say we must from this point on avoid doing any of *the many wrongs that we do*: those obvious non-virtues that anyone can see are mistaken. We must also, though, seek to recognize and abandon even the very *slightest* harms we commit; the ones we barely realize that we do.

The most important thing is for us to follow the words of that King of the Dharma, Dromtun Je:

> We have little time to live,
> It's sure we'll not long be here.
>
> Let the world pass the time
> Working to feed themselves;
> Even the poorest know how.
>
> Those who follow the rules of Dharma
> Need not worry,
> The knife of hunger
> Can never touch and kill them.
>
> Leave this life behind;
> You can't work for the future life
> And for this one as well.
>
> The next is the more important one;
> Make effort in the Dharma.[59]

He says as well,

> Whether you fill your belly
> In this life well or not,
> Still you will live on.

---

[59] *We have little time to live:* These lines appear in *Selections from Dromtun Je.* See ff. 53a–53b of entry B15.

What's difficult is
To meet the Dharma
In your future life;

For this life then
Put all your efforts
Only in the Dharma.

If now you cannot do your best
To do what's virtuous,
Be sure that in the life beyond
You will feel only pain.[60]

And so we have no other choice, if we hope to pass on to one
of the better births in our next life, than to prepare the proper
cause; that is, to do the things we should, and not do what
we shouldn't. There are quite nearly a limitless number of
instructions on how to carry this out—to make it easy for us,
the compassionate Teacher provided a guide of what to take
up and what to give up: this then is the list of ten good deeds
and ten bad deeds, the broadest simplification.[61]

Keeping this morality, of avoiding the ten bad deeds, is
just one typical example *of the many* different kinds of good
that are contained within the broader and the more subtle
instructions on how to go for refuge. We must engage in

---

[60] *You will feel only pain:* Quotation from the same source as the last; see entry
B15, f. 54b.

[61] *The broadest simplification:* The list of ten bad deeds (their avoidance being
the ten good deeds) are a very gross abbreviation of the multitude of harmful
actions which we are capable of performing. They include three which we
perform with our bodies: killing, stealing, and sexual misconduct. The next
four are verbal: lying, divisive talk, harsh words, and idle speech. The final
three are mental: being unhappy when others get something they want; happy
when they get something they don't want; and mistaken views of how the
world works. The classic presentation of the ten is found in the "Chapter on
Deeds" from the *Treasure House of Higher Knowledge;* see ff. 13a–13b, entry S26,
and its commentary by the First Dalai Lama, ff. 127a–127b, entry B11.

each and every one of these virtues by *being ever careful*—by acting with proper recollection and watchfulness in every moment of the day.

And we must go further: on every occasion that we train ourselves in these thoughts—in the Steps which are shared with persons of lesser and medium capacity—we must do so with the ultimate intent of using them as a foundation for training ourselves in the path for those of great capacity.

In short, said our Lama, we must understand how to employ these Steps as a means for developing the Wish for enlightenment. And in these lines we are requesting our Lama to help us find the ability to do so.

Steps Shared with Those
of Medium Capacity

V. Learning How to Want Freedom

With this we have reached the second part in the advices on how to take the essence of this life; that is, how to train one's mind in the Steps of the path which are shared with persons of medium spiritual capacity. Here there are two divisions. The first is learning how to want freedom, and is presented in the single verse of the root text which follows:

(5)

Bless me to perceive
All that's wrong
With the seemingly good things
Of this life.

I can never get enough of them.
They cannot be trusted.
They are the door
To every pain I have.

Grant me then
To strive instead
For the happiness of freedom.

Suppose we are able to follow all the instructions above: we contemplate how death works, and think on the sufferings of the lower realms. Then we make all the effort we are supposed to in going for refuge, and in observing the laws of deeds and their consequences. Admittedly then we could manage, once or twice, to reach one of the better forms of life—as a pleasure being or human—and also acquire some incredible amount of wealth; at least for the time being.

But the nature of all pleasant things in the circle of life is that, no matter how much we get, and no matter how much we enjoy what we get, we *never feel as though we've had enough.* It only makes us want more, it only increases our desire. And this then delivers to us a whole variety of unbearable pain. The pleasant things turn around, and become *the door to every pain I have.*

That highest of Victors, the Great Fifth of the Dalai Lamas, has said as well,

> What happened before?
>> Someone has been in my mind for time
>> with no beginning.
>
> When was that?
>> There's never been a moment when
>> they were gone.
>
> Who are they?
>> I live, and live again, the negative emotions.
>
> And in the end?
>> They will leave me to rot in the ocean of
>> suffering life, without an end in sight.
>
> And the karma?
>> It comes like the wind, with all the
>> things I never wanted.
>
> How far?
>> It whips around me everywhere,
>> and stirs great waves, the three forms
>> of suffering.

How long?
>   I could wander around this sea forever;
>   the torch would spin, and the circle of
>   light would blaze.

What should I see?
>   Think on this, and see that the
>   negativities of the mind are the one
>   true enemy.

What must be done?
>   The enemy of living for this life must die.

Who shall do it?
>   You will have to pretend that you are
>   warrior enough to be the one.

When will it come?
>   Your foes, the negative emotions in
>   your mind, have always been there
>   waiting, ready for the battle.

Now then?
>   The time has surely come: go forth now
>   and defeat them.[62]

---

[62] *Go forth now and defeat them:* These lines are found in the Great Fifth's famous presentation on the Steps of the path, entitled *Word of the Gentle One.* They occur as a poetic interlude between sections of the work's prose philosophical presentation, a device favored as well by His Holiness the First Dalai Lama. See entry B21, ff. 46b–47a.

The "negative emotions" mentioned here constitute a basic source of all our suffering. Their primary characteristic is to disturb our peace of mind, and linguistically as well their name in Sanskrit, *klesha,* comes from a verbal root meaning "to distress." Although the mental afflictions are nearly countless, the six primary ones are ignorant liking, anger, pride, ignorance, harmful doubt, and wrong views. See Prof. Whitney's *Roots of the Sanskrit Language,* entry E11, p. 27; and Kedrup Tenpa Dargye's *Overview of the Perfection of Wisdom,* entry B42, Vol. 1, f. 73a.

As the lines point out, there is one thing which acts as the very root of all our sufferings here in the circle of life. This is none other than the enemy of the negative emotions, so dearly cherished by us, so close to our hearts.

From time with no beginning up to the present moment, this enemy has led us by the hand to all kinds of unbearable pain. And if still we find ourselves unable to discard these bad thoughts once and for all, they will force us to collect karma. Then the karma will force us to take yet another birth in this house, in the circle of suffering life. And there once again the negative emotions will start, and then we'll collect the karma anew. And so it is decided: this karma again will force us into the impure parts of a suffering being, in one of the six forms of life. We'll be born, and then again, and over again and again, wandering through these six.[63]

Once we have taken a birth in the cycle, we'll find ourselves tormented by the three different kinds of suffering, without the slightest break.[64] It doesn't matter at all whether

---

[63] *Six forms of life:* That is, the six different possible types of rebirth: as a hellbeing, a craving spirit, an animal, a human, someone nearly a pleasure being, or a full pleasure being. See also footnote 39 (*Three lower realms,* page 56).

[64] *Three different kinds of suffering:* The illustrious Kedrup Tenpa Dargye explains them as follows in his *Overview of the Perfection of Wisdom:*

> What we call "pervasive" suffering is the subtle condition of change, the fact that the physical, mental, and other parts of ourselves which we have taken on cannot remain, but begin to change from the moment after they come into existence. The suffering of change is typified by the pleasant sensation of the taste of a fine meal. The suffering of suffering, outright suffering, would be something like the painful sensation of a backache.
>
> There is, by the way, a good reason for calling the first of these "pervasive" suffering; for this is a kind of pain which pervades each and every thing produced by karma and negative emotions, and pervades too all three realms of cyclic existence. Moreover, this particular suffering pervades each of the other two kinds.

See f. 70a in Vol. 1 of entry B42.

we take a higher birth or a lower one; there exists no such thing as a pleasant moment here. Whatever place we go is a place that brings us pain. Whatever friend we go with is a friend who brings us pain. Whatever possession we have is a possession which brings us pain. They cannot and will not ever be anything else.

"What way then," you may ask, "must I follow to escape this pain?" You must find a way to stop the stream of births, the circle of life that has karma and the negative emotions as its very nature. Until you manage to do so, you will never find a place that is free of this suffering.

The key to stopping the stream of suffering births is found in the root text of the Three Principal Paths, where the Lord of Lamas says,

> Think over and over how deeds and their
>   fruits never fail,
> And the cycle's suffering: stop desire for
>   the future.[65]

Suppose at first we are able to find the very highest of the supposed good things of this life: we attain the celestial form or fantastic wealth of a god-like being such as Pure One, or Destroyer of a Hundred Cities, or one of those emperors who rules the world with a disk of power. None of these forms can be trusted though, for the inevitable end of each is that we meet the karmic *fruits of bad deeds* we collected before. These deeds throw us into births like those of the lower realms, where we are forced to go through the unlimited variety of pain here in the *cycle of suffering life.*

We must understand this process, and think over and over about all the problems brought to us by the great source

---

[65] *Stop desire for the future:* The quotation is found on f. 194a of Je Rinpoche's classic work on the essentials of Buddhism; see entry B37. The English version is on p. 77, entry E9.

of all pain: ignorant deeds and the negative emotions. We must *stop desire for any future lives.*

Before we can do this we need something else:

> Leisure and fortune are hard to find,
>   life's not long;
> Think it constantly, stop desire for
>   this life.[66]

As the verse says, we must *stop desire for this life first.* To do so, think how *hard it is to find this leisure and fortune.* And think too on the following: while you may have managed just this once to find a perfect body and life, still you must die. *You cannot stay here long*—there is no way to tack on any extra years to your life, and the years you do have leak away constantly, never pausing.

Whatever you and I hope to accomplish—whether it be keeping ourselves out of the three lower realms, or attaining freedom and the state of All-Knowing—we must learn to stop this habit of hoping for the "good" things of this life.

This is absolutely essential all through our Dharma career: from the very beginning, on through the middle, and up to the final end.

These last few points are covered especially well in the works of the new and older schools of the Keepers of the Word, as well as in the texts of the original masters in the Lineage of the Word.[67] If you use these books for training your mind in these Steps, you will have powerful results.

---

[66] *Stop desire for this life:* Also found in the Master's *Three Principal Paths,* entry B37, f. 194a. See also p. 61, entry E9, for the English version.

[67] *Lineage of the Word:* The new and older schools of the Keepers of the Word, the Kadampas, are explained at footnote 29 (*The older Keepers of the Word,* page 41). "Lineage of the Word" is a translation of the word Kagyu, the name of one of the four great traditions of Tibetan Buddhism.

Listen to these descriptions of suffering life, first from the lips of the Victor, Yang Gunpa:

> You can't be sure you will live,
> Nor fix the time you die;
>
> This monster, the Lord of Death,
> Has no interest
> To come at your convenience.
>
> The four elements of your physical body
> And your mind
> Could go today their separate ways;
>
> Think about it:
> Can you ever feel secure,
> Can you ever feel at peace?[68]

He adds other lines including:

> This devil, greed,
> Collected money
>
> Ignoring all discomfort
> And hardship to do so;

---

[68] *You can't be sure you will live:* The Victor Yang Gunpa (1213–1258) was a famed early writer and practitioner of Tibetan Buddhism, and is known for a group of works called the "Hermit Cycle." He is one of the founding fathers of the "Drukpa" or "Dragon" lineage of the tradition of the Kagyu: the "Lineage of the Word." For a full account of his life, see Prof. George N. Roerich's translation of the *Blue Annals,* a history of Buddhism by Shunnu Pel, the Master Translator of Gu, at entry E7, pp. 688–692.

We have not located the original source of these and the following quotations, but this first one also appears in a work by the First Panchen Lama on methods for maintaining one's morality. See f. 6b, entry B58.

But we have no power
To carry even
A bit with us that day.

What's the use of money,
That's never there
When you need it?

Our friends and family
Stayed with us
Through thick and thin;

We won and kept them
By fitting in,
And maintaining our reputation.

But there's not one
Who can take one step
Along with us that day.

What's the use of family, friends,
Who are never there
When you need them?

With toil and sweat
We built a great
And wonderful house for ourselves;

To do it we obliterated
Every rule
Of what to do, or say, or think.

But what happens when
Lord Death decides
He'll not sleep in one morning?

What's the use of a house

That's never there
When you need it?

And then he says,

In the summer
Great clouds crowd the sky,

And lightning comes,
And lightning goes–

The suffering called impermanence
Drags our life
Downhill;

Dispense with the sense
Of permanence,
Of feeling prepared.

The rain brings it on,
The fortuitous moment,
When everything is just right,

And a rainbow comes,
And a rainbow goes—

The suffering called impermanence
Drags our happiness
Downhill;

Dispense with
Looking your best,
And strutting around.

A sudden sound
Brings it on,

And an echo comes,
And an echo goes—

The suffering called impermanence
Drags our fame
Downhill;

Dispense with
The hope for greatness,
The hope for a name.

They travel to the big city
To sell their wares,
And stop in some hotel,

The guest comes in the morning,
The guest leaves in the eve—

The suffering called impermanence
Drags our friends
Downhill;

Dispense with hoping
To fit in with your friends
And family.

In the summertime the bees
Labor and build up
Their hives,

But anyone can see
How they are wiped out
In an instant—

The suffering called impermanence
Drags our food and money
Down the hill.

Dispense with trying
To gather together
All this money and food.

Contemplate on these quotations, and on works like the verses by Drom Gyalway Jungney, where he urges himself to perfect his practice.[69] Think them over constantly, and try your hardest to follow the instructions on how to give up living for this life.

This in itself though is not enough, as expressed in the following words of Kelsang Gyatso, the highest of all the Victors:

This thing they call
The three realms of cyclic life
Is a house of red-hot steel;

Wherever you go
In any of the ten directions,
The suffering will burn you.

You wish so badly
That it weren't happening,
But this is its very nature.

---

[69] *Urges himself to perfect his practice:* A catalog from the Kokonor region of Tibet contains two references to a book entitled *Exhorting Myself to Practice the Dharma with the Magic Tree of Faith,* and states that it was composed by Drom Gyalway Jungney, otherwise known as Dromtun Je—Lord Atisha's foremost disciple. See entry B14; as well as pp. 91 and 632 in *A Catalog of Some of the Great Books of Tibet,* at bibliography entry B79. As this volume was being reprinted in 2023, we received from the Buddhist Digital Research Center (BDRC) the text as found in entry B13.

> How pitiful our life,
> To wander aimlessly
> In such a house of horrors.[70]

This cycle of life, with its three different realms, is absolutely nothing but suffering, by its very nature. It doesn't matter at all whether you take a higher birth within it, or a lower—it's all the same. Consider carefully the truth of these words, then go and seek some way of finding freedom from the cycle, and a way to smash your enemy: the negative emotions.

You and I might have some delusions about getting it all together in this world; a good body, lots of things, power, fame. Regardless of how far we progress in these things though, let's be honest. If we judge ourselves properly, we can see that we aren't really much more advanced in our intellect or strength than common animals—than bugs or birds or whatever.

These things are hardly something worth getting attached to, nothing you would want to hang on to until your dying breath, *nothing you could trust at all.* Much less; for you can even attain the ultimate pleasures and possessions of all cyclic life—you could become the mighty being called Pure One, or Destroyer of a Hundred Cities, or else enjoy all the many riches in the kingdom of a world emperor. In the end though it always turns out the way that the *Letter to a Friend* and other such works describe it: wandering aimlessly around in a house of horrors, the three lower realms of life.

It really doesn't matter what kind of so-called "good" thing you can get here in the world of suffering, eventually all it can do is deceive you. You must by yourself expose the lie; you must learn to think clearly about all the problems

---

[70] *Such a house of horrors:* The lines are found in a beautiful short piece entitled *A Song of Deep Despair,* from a collection of mental trainings by this seventh of the Dalai Lamas. See f. 46a, entry B6. The quotation is also found in Pabongka Rinpoche's *Gift of Liberation,* entry B48, f. 264b.

these things always bring to you. In time you will see, you will know, that every inch of this suffering cycle is in its essence pain.

By then you will have renunciation, the kind that wants to reach the joy of the nirvana beyond both extremes,[71] freedom in the short run from the sufferings of the three lower births, and ultimately from each and every pain in the cycle of life. And it will be the extraordinary form of renunciation, not the rough kind that you get just from following whatever someone else tells you, not the one that stays in the mouth and not the heart—in words and not in truth.

What we are requesting then here, said our Lama, is that our Lama *grant us* the strength to develop a very fierce desire, a strong and genuine wish *to strive for the happiness of freedom*.

---

[71] *Nirvana beyond both extremes:* Refers to the nirvana attained by a fully enlightened Buddha, who eliminates every form of spiritual obstacle, and is thus free of both the extreme of living in the cycle of suffering life, and the extreme of staying in a lower, personal nirvana. See the great Kedrup Tenpa Dargye's *Analysis of the Perfection of Wisdom,* f. 39a, Vol. 1, entry B41.

VI. Finding the Right Path
to Freedom

This brings us to the second division of how to train one's mind in the Steps of the path which are shared with persons of medium spiritual capacity; that is, defining just what kind of path can take us to this freedom. This point is covered in a single verse from the root text:

(6)

Grant that these pure thoughts
May lead me to be watchful
And to recall
What I should be doing,

Grant me to give
The greatest care
To make the vows of morality
The essence of my practice;

They are
The root of the Buddha's teaching.

Up to now we have explained how to truly see that even the supposed good things of the circle of life have no essence at all. When that happens, we begin to feel a total disgust for every corner of the cycle of life. These fierce feelings of renunciation, these pure thoughts where we wish to reach the happiness of freedom, will lead us on to something else, as described by the Omniscient One himself:

> The entire extent
> Of the highest of spoken words,
> The teaching of the Buddhas,
> Is contained in the three collections.
>
> This then is why
> The three different trainings
> Are the essence of the teachings.
>
> These three start
> With the training
> Of morality,
>
> And it's spoken that
> It resides
> In the collection on discipline.
>
> This explains why
> So much of the holy Dharma,
> Spoken so very well,
>
> Was set down in the form
> Of the works
> On discipline.
>
> Could it ever happen then
> That those wise ones
> Who understand
>
> The proper order
> Of the teachings
> Would not take joy in these?

Nowhere does it say
Anything else but this:
If you hope to develop

Insight, the training
Of wisdom well,
You must find quietude,
That of concentration.

It says as well
That if you wish to develop
Pure single-pointed mind,

You must have the training
Of morality;
And this is fine advice.

Some brave souls
Claim they'll keep
A lot of different vows,

But it's oh so common
To see them smash
Whatever pledges they've made.

The way of the holy
Is to strive
To maintain their morality pure,

Exactly as
They have agreed
To do so.

Once you see
The truth in this,
Then use your watchfulness,

Constantly check
Your thoughts, words, and deeds
To stop any wrong to come.

Recollect yourself,
Take the greatest care,
Have a sense of shame,
And consideration;

Use them on
The horse of the senses
When it mistakes the way.

Use your strength
To rein the horse in,
For this is the state of mind

That you can bring
To focus and stay
On any virtuous object

Solidly,
Whatever you want,
However you wish it to be;

And this is why
They sing the praises
Of morality as the way

To reach one-pointedness of mind.[72]

---

[72] *They sing the praises of morality:* The circumstances of the composition of these lines in praise of morality were especially joyful. Je Tsongkapa had sent one of his favorite disciples, Tsako Ngawang Drakpa, to eastern Tibet in order to teach and establish new monasteries. Upon the ordination of the first monks in the area of Gyalmo Rong, the disciple wrote a letter to the Master informing him of the event. These words are from an exquisite epistle which Je Tsongkapa sent in reply. See f. 191b of entry B33.

The process that Je Tsongkapa is describing goes like this. *Recollection* comes at the beginning, and keeps you from forgetting *what you should be doing,* and what you shouldn't be doing. *Watchfulness* then stops by from time to time to check whether or not the activities of your body, speech, and mind are tending towards right or wrong. One's ability to take *great care* in their life functions throughout; it prevents every sort of improper thought or action, and keeps one within the bounds of what is appropriate to undertake.

The essential points of the entire *teaching of the* victorious *Buddha*—the meaning of the contents of the three collections of the Word—all this is included within three precious, extraordinary forms of training: the trainings of morality, of meditative concentration, and wisdom. The crux on which the latter two trainings turn, their basis, *their root* and the ground they stand upon, is in the main a single item: morality, in the form of the various vows of freedom.[73] As the great Panchen Lama, Lobsang Chukyi Gyaltsen, has said,

> It all begins
> When you think to yourself
> "It won't hurt much
>
> If I break a few
> Of these minor vows
> In a minor way";

---

[73] *The various vows of freedom:* Refers to the eight sets of vows found in the Buddhist scriptures; three are for lay people, and five for the ordained. Generally speaking they are called "vows of freedom" because—by observing them carefully—one can reach the freedom of nirvana. Perhaps the clearest and most concise presentation of the eight is found in Je Tsongkapa's own *Essence of the Ocean of Discipline,* at entry B38.

Before too long
You have gone against
A great many of your vows.

If you really think about it,
This kind of attitude
Is like a butcher

Who comes to
Rip out the life
Of your future higher birth.[74]

The point here is that, if something so small as breaking a
single minor vow can escalate so far, then needless to say
when we amass a collection of even greater transgressions
it's only proper that it would eventually lead us precisely
to one of the three lower realms—to a kind of pain which is
totally beyond our ability to withstand it.

For this reason we must be sure never to think lightly of
any transgression we might commit, even down to the minor
vows; we must absolutely keep all our vows just so. And so
you must become masters in understanding all the various
vows and advices related to whichever one of the eight sets
of the vows of freedom you have assented to follow. And
once you have learned them perfectly, well then you must
make them the essence of your practice.

This is what you are requesting, said our Lama, from
your Lama in this verse. You are asking that he or she help
you gain the strength to keep your vows perfectly; that you

---

[74] *Comes to rip out the life:* Lobsang Chukyi Gyaltsen (1567?–1662) was the
first of the great Panchen Lamas and a renowned philosopher, historian, and
statesman—as well as teacher of the great Fifth Dalai Lama. The lines are
found in a short piece entitled *Divine Nectar for Exposing the Harmful Things
I Have Done in the Past, and for Restoring Myself to Spiritual Health, by Relying
on the Antidotes to Bad Deeds, from the Present Moment On.* See entry B56, ff.
269b–270a.

learn to think of the vows contained within your being as the true representative of the Buddha himself, inside you; that you love and cherish your vows, and always hope to defend them. You are asking, he said, to be granted the ability to follow the way of this and the other extraordinary trainings, exactly as they were meant to be.

Open Steps for Those
of Greater Capacity

VII. Developing the Wish for Enlightenment

This brings us to the third and final part of the advices on how to take the essence of this life: how lastly to train one's mind in the Steps of the path for persons of greater spiritual capacity. Here too there are two divisions. The first is how to develop the Wish for enlightenment, and is presented in the single verse of the root text which follows.

(7)

I have slipped and fallen
Into the sea
Of this suffering life;

Bless me to see
That every living being,
Every one my own mother,
Has fallen in too.

Grant me then
To practice this highest
Wish for enlightenment,

To take on myself
The task of freeing them all.

Now the *Sutra That Viradatta Requested* says,

> Were the merit of the Wish for enlightenment
> To take on some kind of physical form
> It would fill the reaches of space itself
> And then spill over farther still.[75]

A Guide to the Bodhisattva's Way of Life too has lines like
the following:

> All the other
> Kinds of virtue
> Are like a bamboo tree;
>
> They give their fruits
> And then they always
> Die and go away.
>
> But the Wish for
> Buddhahood
> Is an evergreen that always
>
> Gives forth its fruits,
> And instead of fading
> Flourishes even more.[76]

---

[75] *Fill the reaches of space itself:* Quotation from f. 352b of this teaching of
the Buddha himself (entry S34). It is also found in Pabongka Rinpoche's
commentary to the *Three Principal Paths,* and in numerous other works on
the Steps to the path. See pp. 95–96 of the commentary's English translation,
entry E9.

[76] *Flourishes even more:* The lines are found on f. 2b of Master Shantideva's
classic manual for bodhisattvas, entry S36.

The Great Lord has also spoken:

> Those great beings
> Who meditate
> On the method,
>
> And so upon
> The various kinds
> Of wisdom,
>
> Achieve then
> Enlightenment
> With speed.
>
> It cannot be done
> By meditating
> On no-self-nature alone.[77]

Our Lord Lama himself says finally,

> The Wish for enlightenment
> Is the central beam
> That holds up every path
> Of the way which is supreme.[78]

We can see from these and other works that the fine qualities of the Wish for enlightenment are limitless. From the first moment that you and I decide we are going to try to reach the state of a Buddha, this Wish for enlightenment is something we can never do without.

---

[77] *Those great beings who meditate:* The verses are from the *Lamp on the Path,* Lord Atisha's famed prototype for Tibetan texts on the Steps to Buddhahood. They are also quoted in the early *Steps of the Teaching* by Geshe Drolungpa. See f. 240a, entry S1, and f. 346b, entry B55.

[78] *The Wish for enlightenment is the central beam:* The verse appears in Je Tsongkapa's *Songs of My Spiritual Life.* See f. 56b, entry B30.

The minute we reach this state of mind, we win the title of "Daughter" or "Son" of the Buddha, even if we have no other admirable qualities at all. We also then enter the ranks of people who live the greater way.

If though we lack this great Wish, then it doesn't matter how many great virtues we might possess—abilities like being able to meditate on the ultimate view, where we see that things have no nature of their own. We still won't be able to join the ranks of those on the greater way, much less reach enlightenment. And so the Wish is vital.

In the sections where we trained ourselves in the steps that are shared with practitioners of lesser and medium capacity, we meditated on the sufferings of the lower realms, and of the entire circle of life, but relative only to ourselves. In this way we developed the virtue of a healthy disgust for the kind of life we live.

Here you take the same thoughts and transfer them—you try to feel them relative to the condition that others are in. Then compassion and the other attitudes will start to grow within you; train your mind thus in the proper progression, using either the "seven-part, cause-and-effect instruction," or else the practice called "exchanging self and others," following these methods as the books on the Steps of the path to Buddhahood describe them.[79]

---

[79] *Train your mind in the proper progression:* The texts on the Steps to Buddhahood state that the great Wish for enlightenment can equally be developed by using either of the methods mentioned. The "seven-part, cause-and-effect instruction" comes down to us from Lord Buddha through masters such as Chandrakirti, Chandragomi, and Shantarakshita. It involves a preliminary step, developing neutrality towards all other beings, and then seven parts, the last being a result of the first six. The seven are:

1) Recognize that all beings have, in past lives, been your own mother.

2) Contemplate the kindness they showed you.

3) Develop a desire to repay them.

4) Find a kind of love where every other living being looks as lovely to you as a mother's only child.

You must train yourself in all the relevant details; an example would be committing yourself through formal rituals to the Wish as a prayer and to the Wish as actual action, once you had reached a point such as finding your first strong feelings of familiarity with the Wish.

The meaning of the root text here then is as follows. *I* myself *have slipped and fallen into the sea* of the pain *of this suffering life;* that is, I have dropped into the ocean of the circle of births. I cannot even guess how deep it is, nor how far its edges lie. The great sea-waves of my deeds and negative emotions, of birth and getting old and death, rage around me.

A great host of ruthless creatures living in the water rise up and attack me constantly; these are the three sufferings— the suffering of outright pain, the suffering of pleasure that changes, and the suffering of simply being alive. They rip at me, they torture me, relentlessly, unceasingly.

And the same thing is happening to *every* other *living being. Every one* of them has in the past been *my own mother;* in the beginningless string of lives I have lived through, they cared for me and sheltered me, with incredible kindness.

I must learn *to see* how all these fellow beings *have fallen in too,* how they have been thrown down into misery by this mass of suffering. And then I must resolve *to take upon myself the task of freeing them all* from every pain, and from every cause of pain. I must assure they reach every form

---

5) Feel a strong compassion for them, a wish that they could escape every kind of pain.

6) Resolve to help them escape, through your own personal effort, by any means necessary.

7) This then brings you to the Wish to achieve enlightenment for the sake of every living being.

The practice of "exchanging self and others" comes down to us from the Buddha through Master Shantideva, and means to replace one's concern for our own welfare with a concern for the welfare of others. Both methods combine in the teachings of Lord Atisha, Je Tsongkapa, and the Lamas of their lineage. See Pabongka Rinpoche's *Gift of Liberation,* entry B48, f. 300a*ff.*

of happiness. I will do it myself, alone, without waiting or depending on anyone else. Beyond everything, I myself will see to it that every one of them climbs to the state of a Buddha.

In short, said our Lama, we are asking our Lama for the ability to find fierce feelings of love and compassion, states of mind where we can bear not a moment longer to watch our fellow, mother beings live so bereft of happiness, and so plagued by suffering. We are asking that these feelings inspire in us the *highest* aspiration, the true and uncontrived *Wish for enlightenment.* And we are asking our Lama for the ability to meditate upon this Wish, and *practice* it, and make it totally perfect, right here, on this very seat, before we stand up again.

VIII. General Training in
Bodhisattva Activities

With this we have reached the second division to the
instruction on how to train one's mind in the Steps of the
path for persons of greater spiritual capacity. This division
covers training yourself in the activities of a bodhisattva, once
you have managed to achieve the Wish for enlightenment
just described.

Our discussion proceeds in two parts: training in the
open half of the bodhisattva activities, and training in the
secret half of the bodhisattva activities. The former has two
steps as well; the first of these explains how to train oneself
in the activities as a whole, and is presented in a single verse
of the root text.

(8)

Bless me to see clearly
That the Wish itself
Is not enough,

For if I'm not well trained
In the three moralities,
I cannot become a Buddha.

Grant me then
A fierce resolve
To master the vows
For children of the Victors.

Suppose you are able, as described above, to reach *the Wish* for enlightenment, where you truly hope to achieve the state of a Buddha in order to help every living being. This *itself is not enough.* Once you do reach the Wish, you must still take on the vows of these bodhisattva princesses and princes, these sons and daughters of the victorious Buddhas. And then you must train yourself in giving and the other five perfections. Otherwise there is no way you could ever come to enlightenment.

This fact explains why it is so very important when holy beings have said that all six perfections[80] are covered in the three types of morality.

The first type is called the "morality of keeping oneself from committing wrong." Here you begin by being extremely careful to keep the morality of avoiding the ten bad deeds.[81] This type of good behavior is common to everyone, whether they wear the robes or not, and must absolutely be maintained.

More specifically, with this first type of morality, you must in addition exert yourself to the fullest, so to assure that your life is never sullied in the least by overstepping the bounds of any of the vows you have agreed to keep. Here we refer to vows that belong to any of the three traditional sets: the freedom vows, the bodhisattva vows, and the secret vows.[82]

---

[80] *All six perfections:* The six Buddhist perfections are giving, morality, controlling anger, enjoying good deeds, meditative concentration, and wisdom. One important source for the six is Master Chandrakirti's *Entering the Middle Way,* with chapters devoted to each. See entry S9.

[81] *Avoiding the ten bad deeds:* See footnote 61 (*The broadest simplification,* page 78) for the ten.

[82] *Three sets of vows:* The freedom vows have been discussed above; see footnote 73 (*The various vows of freedom,* page 83). The bodhisattva vows consist of 18 root vows and 46 secondary vows, by which one commits him- or herself to the service of other beings. The secret vows are undertaken for the purpose of attaining enlightenment in this life, in order to benefit all sentient kind. See Pabongka Rinpoche's *Gift of Liberation,* entry B48, f. 383b.

The second type of morality is known as the "morality of collecting goodness." This is where you use a great variety of means to gather or collect extremely potent stores of virtue into your being; these are the virtues of amassing merit and wisdom.[83]

The third type of morality is the "morality that acts for every living being." Here you take care to keep the different varieties of morality mentioned above that involve restraining yourself from wrong; but instead of doing so with a motivation which is infected with any self-interest, you act only out of an intention to reach total Buddhahood for the sake of all living kind.

You must find a sure kind of knowledge where you see clearly how—if you lack a total fluency in *these three types of morality,* if you are not *well trained* and completely accustomed to following them—then you *cannot become* one of those who has reached the fully enlightened state of a *Buddha.*

Once you have found this knowledge, you must take on *the vows for the "children of the Victors"* (that is, the bodhisattva vows), and then with a *resolve* of *fierce* intensity you must learn and master the three types of morality. What we are requesting of our Lama here, said our Lama, is that she or he grant us the ability to do so.

---

[83] *Amassing merit and wisdom:* These two huge collections of good deeds and knowledge within one's mind stream act as the causes for the physical form and the omniscient state of a Buddha, respectively. See Pabongka Rinpoche's commentary to Je Tsongkapa's *Three Principal Paths,* entry B47, f. 4a (English translation at entry B119, p. 36).

IX. Training in the Final Two
Perfections

Having presented the bodhisattva activities in general, we will now turn to the more particular description of how to train oneself in the final two perfections. This point is covered in the single verse of the root text which follows.

(9)

Grant that I may quickly gain
The path where quietude
And insight join together;

One which quiets
My mind from being
Distracted to wrong objects,

The other which analyzes
The perfect meaning
In the correct way.

The verse here speaks of objects which are "wrong"; this should be understood as referring to objects which are mistaken, in a particular sense. One example would be trying to develop meditative concentration by fixing the mind on a short stick of wood, as some non-Buddhists advocate. We must seek to *"quiet" the mind*—that is stop the mind—*from being distracted to* these types of *wrong*, external *objects*.

There are Tibetan schools of the past too which have taught that meditative quietude consists of not thinking about anything at all, just keeping the mind in some dark state of dullness. The high state of perfect insight then they explain as moving in this stupor to a realization of the pure and simple emptiness of the deceptive nature of the mind—except they describe this emptiness as what you come to when you analyze whether or not what we call the "mind" consists of any shape or color, and then fail to find that it's any such thing.

But none of these ideas is correct; rather, we must follow texts such as the briefer and more expanded explanations of the Steps to the path composed by the Lord himself, where he presents the instructions given by the Great Regent, Loving One, in his own work entitled *Separating the Middle and the Extremes.*

These treatises describe how one progresses in steps by eliminating the five problems to meditation, taking the eight corrective actions, and achieving the nine mental states, complete with their four different modes.[84]

---

[84] *Five problems to meditation:* The texts on the Steps to Buddhahood describe in detail the concept of five problems which occur as a person attempts to develop the perfect concentration known as "meditative quietude." These five are countered by eight corrective measures, and lead the meditator through nine different states, with four modes. *Separating the Middle and the Extremes* is one of the works granted to Master Asanga in the 4th century by Maitreya, the future Buddha. It outlines these components of meditation in a very brief way and is used as the basis for later presentations. See entry S24, f. 41a.

The first of the five problems is called "laziness," a lack of motivation even to sit down and start trying to develop perfect concentration. It is countered by the first four of the corrective measures. Here one begins by developing (1) "faith," which means a clear understanding of the benefits of concentration. Once they are aware of these benefits, the meditator begins to (2) "aspire" to achieve them, which provides the impetus for (3) great "effort." The result of these three is (4) a kind of physical and mental "pliancy" which allows one to meditate easily. Practicing then becomes enjoyable, which is a natural antidote for the initial hesitation to begin meditating.

The second of the problems likely to arise in meditation is "forgetting the instruction," which here refers to losing the object which one has chosen to meditate upon. The correction for this is "remembering," which means trying to keep the mind on the object tightly, as you would hold a rope to keep it from slipping.

Only now, once the object is within one's mental grasp, can the third problem occur: dullness and agitation. Dullness is a heaviness of body and mind; in its gross form, one succeeds in fixing the mind but has no clarity—none of the bright, focused feeling one gets for example while concentrating on a good book. With the subtle form of dullness one enjoys both fixation and clarity, but the clarity lacks intensity. This leads to perhaps the most common error in meditation, marked by long periods of dimly focused dullness, a fuzzy good feeling easily mistaken for real concentration.

Agitation, the second part of the third problem, occurs when the mind is distracted to an attractive object. The correction for both sides of the problem is known as "mindfulness," which simply means watching your own mind to catch yourself turning dull or agitated.

Although mindfulness may detect a problem occurring during meditation, one might fail to act upon the alarm, and this is the fourth problem. It is overcome by taking action, by tightening down on the meditation object in the case of subtle dullness, and by lightening up when this goes too far and causes a reaction of agitation. The idea is to maintain the proper tension, like tuning a guitar string: not too loose, and not too tight. The correction swings to either side of the problem, whichever necessary, as the driver of a car constantly corrects to left and right in order to keep a straight line.

At some point a straight line is achieved, and the concentration is running fine on its own. Now the fifth problem can occur: the fault of correcting when there is nothing to correct. This problem's natural antidote—the eighth—is to leave things alone.

The meditator passes through nine different states during the above process:

1) Fixing the mind: Moments of fixation on the object, with no continuity. Time off the object is more than time on the object.

2) Fixing the mind continuously: Some ability to keep the mind on the object for a continuous period. During these first two states, the mind is in the first of the four modes: engaging only with a conscious effort to focus.

3) Fixing the mind with patches: Mind kept on the object for longer periods, with brief gaps which are quickly patched.

4) Fixing the mind closely: No longer possible to lose the object, but dullness and agitation still very strong.

5) Controlling the mind: Gross dullness and agitation are overcome. Special problems with subtle dullness due to excessive effort to focus the mind inward.

One thus attains a kind of bliss, a total pliancy of body and mind, which comes from staying in one-pointed meditation on any virtuous object one chooses. This then leads to what we call meditative *quietude.*

The phrase *"perfect meaning"* here in the verse refers to a particular object: the fact that nothing has any nature of its own.[85] A kind of wisdom used for examining the nature of something *analyzes* this object *in* a certain *correct way,* and by the end of its analysis comes to a definite conclusion. The mind stays in meditation upon this truth, such that the analysis and a fixation on this object *join* and work *together.* This brings on a feeling of bliss that fills the mind completely—and one has thus achieved what we call "perfect *insight."*

---

6) Stilling the mind: Special problems with subtle agitation due to steps taken to stop subtle dullness.

7) Stilling the mind completely: With few exceptions, all dullness and agitation stopped. Infrequent occurrences of the two are countered by application of effort. During these last five states, the mind is in the second of the four modes: engaging but with interruptions, caused by dullness and agitation.

8) Focusing the mind single-pointedly: Slight initial effort is enough to prevent dullness and agitation for the entire remaining length of a meditation session. During this eighth state, the mind is in the third of the four modes: engaging without interruptions.

9) Balancing the mind: No effort at all required to start and remain in deep, single-pointed meditation.

During the ninth state the mind is in the last of the four modes: engaging effortlessly. This last state is also known as "approximate quietude"; it becomes true meditative quietude when one achieves true physical and mental pliancy.

The preceding discussion is based on Pabongka Rinpoche's *Gift of Liberation,* ff. 348a–358b, entry B48, with additional material from Je Tsongkapa's *Greater Steps,* f. 346b, entry B26.

[85] *The fact that nothing has any nature of its own:* This refers to the Buddhist concept of emptiness, or voidness, and is easily misunderstood. For a full discussion, see Pabongka Rinpoche's own explanation in his commentary to Je Tsongkapa's *Principal Teachings of Buddhism* (English translation), entry E9, pp. 109–133.

We seek to practice this process, where quietude and insight are no longer separated one from the other. When we recite the verse we are asking our Lama to *grant that*, as a result, *we may quickly gain* within our minds that exceptional form of realization where meditative quietude and perfect insight join together.

Secret Steps for Those
of Greater Capacity

X. Entering the Way of the Diamond

This brings us to the second part of our discussion about the activities of a bodhisattva: training oneself in the secret half of these endeavors. Here there are three different Steps: how to enter into the Way of the Diamond by making oneself a worthy vessel, and then receiving a pure form of the four empowerments; how to keep pure the pledges and vows that one took on when they received the empowerments; and how to meditate upon the two stages of this path, as one continues to maintain their pledges and vows. The first of these three is presented in the single verse of the root text which follows.

(10)

Grant that once I've practiced well
The paths shared and become
A vessel that is worthy,

I enter with perfect ease
The Way of the Diamond,

Highest of all ways,
Holiest door to come inside
For the fortunate and the good.

You must first have *practiced well* the general Steps of *the path* which are "*shared*" by both the open and the secret teachings; that is, which are so important for both that you could never succeed without them. More specifically, you must have trained your mind well in the three principal paths: renunciation, the Wish for enlightenment, and the correct view of reality.[86] On top of this you must have as your motivation a very fierce desire to reach enlightenment for the sake of every living being. These then make you a *vessel that is worthy to enter* the Way of the Secret Word.

When this time has come you must surely enter the "*Way of the Diamond*"; which is to say, the Way of the Secret Word. It is the *highest of all* the "different *ways*"—the ways of the listeners, the self-made buddhas, and the bodhisattvas.[87] What makes the Diamond Way higher is that it has certain unique features, such as using the goal of practice as a path to the goal.

The Tibetan word for "diamond" here is *dorje*. This is a translation of the Sanskrit word *vajra*—a term that has the basic meaning of "inseparable." The "diamond" here is the actual diamond of the holy mind of the Buddha: that deep state of meditation which can only be compared to a diamond. You can also say it refers to that one type of wisdom which is the inseparable combination of what we call "method" (great bliss) and "wisdom" (emptiness).

The word for "way" here has a meaning of "conveyance"—something you get on and ride to reach a destination. The "diamond way" mentioned here is thus a kind of "diamond conveyance" as well. In the way of the perfections, one must

---

[86] *The three principal paths:* These three constitute an essential background, without which the study of the *Mountain of Blessings* would be incomplete. They are presented fully in Pabongka Rinpoche's elucidation of Je Tsongkapa's work entitled the *Three Principal Paths;* see B47 (Tibetan original) and E9 (English translation).

[87] *Listeners, self-made buddhas, and bodhisattvas:* See footnote 15 (*One of those foe destroyers,* page 30).

carry on their practice for three "countless" eons in order to reach Buddhahood.[88] This takes so long that it's almost as if you were walking on foot, rather than traveling on any sort of conveyance.

If though you use the Diamond Way, the Way of the Secret Word, no such length of time is needed: you can attain the state of secret Buddhahood, Union, in the length of but one lifetime—even in one of the very short kinds of life that we have here now, in the age of degeneration. In fact it's possible to reach Buddhahood in no more than three years and three months. This way then is a method which is incredibly deep and quick; more like riding a fine racehorse.

The kinds of practitioners that we call "listeners" and "self-made buddhas" aspire only to reach a state of blissful peace, and this too only for themselves. They are deficient therefore in that fortunate kind of good virtue that makes one want to take on the burden of helping others. Bodhisattvas, on the other hand, disregard completely their own comfort and work only for the good of others. They are full of the wonderful fortune and goodness that enable them to reach the state of a perfect Buddha, and the ability to fulfill, totally, the ultimate needs of both others and themselves.

What is the *"holiest"* (meaning highest) *door*, or gateway, for bodhisattvas—for these people who are so *fortunate and good—to come inside* this path? It is receiving the four empowerments of the Diamond Way, the Way of the Secret Word, and receiving them perfectly, so that they are sure to plant the seeds for the four bodies of a Buddha.

What we are requesting in this verse then, said our Lama, is that our Lama grant us the ability to enter, *with perfect ease*, the profound path just described: the Way of the Diamond, the unsurpassed form of the Secret Word.

---

[88] *Three "countless" periods of years:* The word "countless" here actually refers to a specific number—1,000,000,000,000,000,000,000,000,000,000,000, 000,000,000,000,000. The length of an "eon" is variously described in Buddhist scripture, and is tied to cycles in the lifespans of beings; suffice to say it entails many millions of years.

XI. Keeping Vows & Pledges Pure

With this we have reached the second Step to training oneself in the secret half of the bodhisattva activities; that is, how to keep pure the pledges and vows that one took on when he or she received their secret empowerment. This Step too is presented in a single verse of the root text:

(11)

Bless me to know
With genuine certainty
That when I've entered thus,
The cause that gives me
Both the attainments

Is keeping my pledges
And vows most pure.

Grant me then
To always keep them
Even if it costs my life.

Now suppose you *have entered thus*—you have made yourself a vessel which is worthy of the Diamond Way, the Way of the Secret Word; and you have received, in the proper manner, the four different empowerments. If you then follow the correct method you can gain *both the attainments*: the one we call the "ultimate," and the one we describe as "shared."

The ultimate attainment is reaching secret Union, where there is nothing more to be learned. This is the state of the Victorious One, the Keeper of the Diamond.

The shared attainments are those such as the "eight great attainments." These include the special powers known as the sword, the eye ointment, swift feet, the pill, passing underground, disappearing, taking essence, and sky walking.[89]

What then is it that can *give* you these attainments? Their *cause* or foundation, the very support that holds them all up, is one thing, and only one: to *keep most pure* every one of the root and secondary *pledges and vows* which you took upon yourself when you were granted the empowerments.

We must therefore honor and keep, just as we are required, the various vows and pledges. For the bodhisattva vows, this means never committing any of the 18 root downfalls, or the 46 secondary violations. For the secret vows, it involves avoiding perfectly the 14 root downfalls and the eight serious offenses, while being sure to honor the general and also the individual pledges of the Five Classes.

You will never be able to protect all your pledges and vows unless you manage to slam shut the four doors through which the downfalls make their appearance. These four are ignorance, disrespect, carelessness, and particularly severe negative emotions.

---

[89] *Eight great attainments:* These are to gain "the sword," which allows one to travel anywhere; "the pill," which enables you to become invisible or assume any outer form; "the eye ointment," which helps you see minute or very distant objects; "swift feet," the ability to travel at high speeds; "taking essence," an ability to live off nothing but tiny bits of sustenance; "sky walk," the ability to fly; "disappearing," or invisibility; and "underground," the power to pass through solid ground like a fish through water. The *Great Dictionary* describes each of the eight in a separate entry; see bibliography item B80, pp. 2668, 2705, 2091, 88, 755, 298, 2073, and 2907, respectively. An expanded presentation of these attainments is found on ff. 286b–287a of Lord Atisha's autocommentary to *Light on the Path,* entry S2.

To keep these doors closed we must, respectively, learn and know when and how a downfall occurs. We must contemplate the laws of actions & their consequences, thereby gaining a deep respect for the various instructions on how to keep these commitments. We must remain in a constant state of recollection and watchfulness. Finally, we must employ the antidote that will work against the particular negative emotions that happen to be our own most serious problem.

As for where to find instructions on the vows and pledges, you can use a number of works by the Lord, Tsongkapa. Some examples would be his treatise called *Highway to Buddhahood* for advice on the bodhisattva vows, or the *Golden Harvest of Attainments* for a complete explanation of the root downfalls in the secret vows.[90]

At the very least you should study the book of advices on the three sets of vows known as the *String of Shining Jewels*, or one of those summaries in verse that teach about the secret and bodhisattva vows.[91] Use any of these presentations, brief or long, according to the time you have available to you; come to a firm understanding of each of the vows and pledges; and then at all costs keep them.

Let's say you are able to keep your vows and pledges as described—you live your life in proper accordance with them all. Certain results will follow then, even if you find yourself unable to make great efforts in practices such as meditation on the stages of creation & completion, and so therefore fail during this life to reach the final end of the various paths and levels.

---

[90] *A number of works by the Lord*: Je Tsongkapa's classic presentations of the higher vows are found at entries B31 and B39, respectively.

[91] *The secret and bodhisattva vows:* Summaries of these higher vows are found in many of the texts for daily recitation, such as the *Practice for Six Times a Day*. The book of advice mentioned above, the *String of Shining Jewels*, is a concise, exquisite piece by Geshe Tsewang Samdrup of Drepung Monastery, who wrote around 1835 (see entry B67).

The immense power of the purity of your pledges and vows will lead you over the string of your future lives to attain a very special kind of life, where you can practice the secret teachings. You will always meet an authentic Diamond Master—one who teaches you the secret way. And you will always find yourself able to put the secret paths into actual practice.

As such you will, without a doubt, be able to reach total enlightenment within seven lifetimes, or in sixteen at the very most. On this our Teacher, the Keeper of the Diamond, has spoken the following in the *Tantra of the Treasure of Secrets*:

> If the person is granted
> A pure empowerment,
>
> Then life after life
> Will the power be given.
>
> Within seven lives
> The goal is reached,
>
> Even if the person
> Does not meditate.
>
> But those who keep
> The meditation,
>
> And further maintain
> Their pledges and vows,
>
> Will reach the goal
> Within this life or,

Past deeds preventing,
At least in the next.[92]

Vibhuti Chandra says as well,

Even should they fail to meditate,
A person will reach the goal
Within the length of sixteen lives,
So long as a downfall has not occurred.[93]

The *Book of the Five Pledges* concurs:

As long as there is no downfall,
The goal is reached in sixteen lives.[94]

---

[92] *Within seven lives this person will reach:* Je Tsongkapa, in the *Golden Harvest of Attainments* just mentioned, also uses this quotation (see f. 50a, entry B39). He mentions his source as a reference to the *Treasure* within Master Saraha's *Difficult Points on the Secret Teaching of the Skull.* The citation is found there on ff. 144b–145a, entry S37.

[93] *Within the length of sixteen lives:* The quotation is from the *String of Light for the Three Kinds of Vows,* a short piece by Master Vibhuti Chandra found in the Tengyur collection of early Indian commentaries (see f. 54b, entry S27). The lines just preceding those here, by the way, state that:

If they also do their meditation,
A person will reach enlightenment
Here in the very same life.

Je Tsongkapa cites the lines on the sixteen lives in both his *Golden Harvest* and in an epistle sent to a disciple named Kashi Dzinpa, Sherab Pel Sangpo. The great scholar of the secret teachings, Shaluwa Rinchen Lobsang Kyenrab (late 19th century), also speaks of the maximum of sixteen lifetimes. See f. 50a, entry B39; f. 175b, entry B28; and f. 66b, entry B71, respectively.

[94] *The goal is reached:* The quotation is found on f. 30b of this work from the secret teachings of the Tengyur collection (entry S20). Je Tsongkapa again cites the lines as well on f. 50a of his *Golden Harvest* (entry B39)—and again the following words are included in the original:

By force of meditation and the like
A person achieves the goal in this same life.

You must come to *know* these facts *with genuine certainty*—that is, you must seek a kind of firm belief in them that is deeply rooted within you, so much that no one else could ever change your mind. And because of this knowledge you must then protect your commitments, *"even if it costs your life."*

What would it be to cost your life? Imagine for example some follower of a non-Buddhist religion, or some kind of barbarian, who was really very cruel, very evil. And suppose they came up to you and said, "If you don't agree not to keep those pledges and vows of yours, then I swear I will kill you, this very instant." Suppose it were completely decided: either you reject this morality, or you die.

At the "cost of your life" then your choice would go like this. If I discard my morality now they will spare me; but the ultimate hope of my infinite lifetimes will be murdered instead. It's really the same as being killed myself. If though I can keep my morality I will reach the happiness that I've lived all these lives to find. So if to keep my morality now I must let them kill me, then let it be so. I will never give up these morals.

In short, if it comes down to choosing between giving up your life, and letting this morality degenerate, you had surely better choose the first. The one thing here in this birth that you cherish above all else is your own life. What you are requesting from your Lama is that he or she *grant you* the power to *always keep* your vows and pledges properly; that you reach a point where you cherish these commitments infinitely more than your own precious life.

XII. Meditating on the Two
Secret Stages

This brings us to the third Step of training oneself in the secret half of the bodhisattva activities, which is how to meditate upon the two stages of this path, while one continues to maintain her or his pledges and vows. This Step too is presented in a single verse of the root text.

(12)

Bless me next
To realize precisely
The crucial points
Of both the stages,

The essence of
The secret ways.

Grant me then
To practice as
The Holy One has spoken,

Putting all my effort in
And never leaving off
The Practice of the Four Times,
Highest that there is.

One may wonder, "Suppose I am able to maintain my vows and pledges; what must I do after that?" The highest of Victors, Kelsang Gyatso, has spoken the following:

> The point
>> May be birth or death or
>> the state between them.

> The time
>> Most important for planting their seeds
>> is now.

> The way
>> To transform them is the practice of
>> creation & completion.

> The refuge
>> You must learn is
>> the three final bodies themselves.[95]

What's being said here is that, first of all, you must continue to keep each and every one of the secret vows and pledges, as explained above. Then you must practice the very *essence* of the great sea *of the secret ways*. Here first is the stage of creation, which is exemplified by a number of methods.

We tend to see things in an ordinary way, we take them to be no more than what they seem to us; we tend to grasp this way to the place where we live, to our own body, to the things we own and use, and to things like the parts that make up us and the world: what we call the "heaps," the "categories," and the "doors of sense."[96] We have also

---

[95] *Birth or death or the state between:* The lines by His Holiness the Seventh Dalai Lama are found in a letter of advice to one Rabjampa Gendun Drakpa. See f. 32b, entry B6.

[96] *The "heaps," the "categories," and the "doors of sense":* These are three ways of dividing the parts to ourselves and our world; the classic presentation of them

always had to undergo an ordinary birth, ordinary death, and ordinary passage between death and birth.

In the stage of creation we transform all these seemingly ordinary things and events; we turn them into the three bodies of a victorious Buddha.[97] We take whatever presents itself to us: all that appears to our eyes, all that reaches our ears, and all that comes in our thoughts, and we make it show itself as total and absolute purity, as a galaxy of perfection, as great celestial mansions, as holy angels, as a magical dance put on by our Lamas.

As for the stage of completion, some mistakenly equate it with concentrating solely on a meditation that involves the various channels and winds, and which results in achieving a rather ordinary kind of inner heat. Others make the error of thinking it is some high spiritual path where you succeed in nothing more than perceiving how the essence of the mind is that it is aware and knowing.

---

is found throughout the first chapter of Master Vasubandhu's *Treasure House of Knowledge*. See entry S26, ff. 2a–4a, and the commentary of the First Dalai Lama, entry B11, ff. 1b–42a.

The five "heaps" consist of our physical form; our feelings; our ability to discriminate; parts of us not covered in the other four heaps; and our consciousness. They are called "heaps" because each one consists of a large group of different things.

The eighteen "categories" are our five physical senses and our mental sense, along with the corresponding six objects and six consciousnesses. (For example, the physical sense of the eye, visual objects, and consciousness of what we see.) They are called "categories" in the sense of "types." The twelve "doors of sense" are the six senses and their six objects. They are "doors of sense" in that they provide a cause or doorway through which the six types of consciousness arise. These three different presentations of the divisions to us and our world are made to fit varying types of students.

[97] *Three bodies of a victorious Buddha:* The three bodies or parts of a Buddha are known as the Dharma Body, the Body of Enjoyment, and the Body of Emanation. The Dharma Body consists of the Buddha's omniscience; his or her state of having ended all impure qualities; and his or her emptiness. The Body of Enjoyment is the physical body of the Buddha in their paradise, and the Body of Emanation is the form which they project to this and other planets to help living beings. For the technical definitions of the three, see Kedrup Tenpa Dargye, entry B42, Vol 1, f. 47a; Vol 8, f. 17a; and the same volume, f. 18b, respectively.

The real stage of completion though is not like this; rather, you take the various winds which course through the body because of one's ordinary conceptual thinking, and redirect them all into the central channel—in a three-fold process of entrance, residence, and absorption. As a result a primal state of mind arises—the clear light, the wisdom which is simultaneous. And the power of this wisdom makes all of existence appear as the play of bliss and emptiness.

In the path of the stage of creation then we meditate over & over on this and related practices, until finally we are able to bring about the Union of the holy body and holy mind: we reach the state of the Lord of the Secret World, the Keeper of the Diamond.

All this makes it clear why we must study, and study well, the path that includes *both the* secret *stages.* We will have *to realize* all the crucial points of how to actually carry out these two stages. Our understanding must be unerring; it must conform *precisely* with the true intent of the Teacher, as revealed in the secret texts, and the explanations of great and accomplished masters.

Then we must *put forth all our efforts;* that is, we must exert ourselves continually and steadily, to the proper degree—not overdoing it, and not underdoing it. These efforts should go towards following *the Practice of the Four Times* of the day: daybreak, morning, afternoon, and the early night. We must make this practice the single *highest* activity *that there is* in our lives, and try *never to leave off* doing it.

Now there are false teachings that some persons simply make up on their own, out of an ignorant desire for gain. There are paths that are absolutely backwards, and there are paths that will lead you astray. There are paths that are infected by mistaken concepts from an old local religion, or from some non-Buddhist faiths of ancient India, or anything of the like.

What we are requesting of our Lama here, said our Lama, is that he or she *grant us* the power never to wander onto one of these paths. We are asking for the strength to practice, in exactly the proper way, the instructions found in the highest of *spoken* words. And these are the teachings of the "*Holy One*" mentioned in the verse. These words refer to a person who can never deceive us; a being who is incapable of lying; that ultimate meditator who keeps the practice of the times: they refer to the victorious, transcendent Buddha.

In Conclusion

XIII. A Request for Good Circumstances

This brings us to the third major division of the text, which is a request so that we can attain all the favorable conditions for succeeding in the path, and also stop all those circumstances that might keep us from success. This request is contained in the single verse of the root text which follows.

(13)

Bless me, grant me that
The spiritual Guide
Who shows me this good road,

And all my true
Companions in this quest
Live long and fruitful lives.

Bless and grant me that
The rain of obstacles,

Things within me
Or outside me
That could stop me now,
Stop and end forever.

So there are these different sorts of spiritual paths, of widely varying quality: some are totally correct, some are totally wrong, some slide off from right to wrong, and on and on. You and I have access to a path which is pure, and unmistaken, and free of any error. We can either enter it now or go off on some wrong road that goes astray. If this second is our choice then we can try to follow such a way for a thousand years, but it is an absolute impossibility that we will derive from it any good or certain result.

The Great Fifth Dalai Lama has said,

> It's quite nice when you consider
> A teaching to be of your school
> When the Lama who teaches it wears
> A silk cap with the saffron stain.
>
> But remember many are robbed
> By the thief of wandering thoughts,
> Left empty-handed of riches,
> The unique word and the realizations
> Passed down the Family line.[98]

These lines describe people in our school whose knowledge is so little that the only difference they can see between followers of traditions such as the Lineage of the Word or the Ancient Ones, and the tradition of the Virtuous Way, is that some wear lama hats which are red and others wear caps of yellow. People like this are unable to cite a single one of the unique, profound features that distinguish the physical word and the mental realizations of our teachings from those of the other traditions. These people are a disgrace to our school.

Don't let yourself be one of these. For once in your many lifetimes you have met up with a truly pure system, a school like purified gold. The beliefs that it teaches have

---

[98] *But remember many are robbed:* The lines are found in his famed work on the Steps to Buddhahood entitled *Word of the Gentle One.* See entry B21, f. 93a.

been perfectly refined and assayed, like gold that has been through the fire, the shears, and the file. These tests have been carried out with endless hardships by our Gentle Protector, Tsongkapa the Great, who has delivered to us this precious essence of the teachings of the powerful beings of Enlightenment.

We have met with this system, and we must see that a real meeting takes place. We must find and take ourselves properly to a spiritual Guide, one who is truly qualified, and who follows our tradition perfectly in both their viewpoint and their practice. We should undertake to study the five great classics, the five great volumes of the Word, and bring this study to its final end, thereby coming to a firm and accurate understanding of how the two levels of reality work.[99]

We must examine and resolve every question about how to put into practice within our own lives that path where method & wisdom are ever inseparable. We must, in short, ask for and receive teachings on the immaculate system of the greater way; we must learn the various clarifications of these teachings by our Lord Lama and his spiritual Sons, and by those who have come after them; and we must hear the private advices passed along in the oral tradition. And then finally we should use the traditional method to master these teachings, in the three steps of learning, contemplation, and meditation—each one always combined with the others.

---

[99] *How the two levels of reality work:* The five great books have been described above at footnote 24 (*The five great classics,* page 38). The "two levels of reality" refer to what are usually called "deceptive truth" and "ultimate truth." Both are valid, and all objects have both. The dependence of objects (especially in the sense of depending upon the names and concepts we apply to them) is their conventional or deceptive truth. Their appearance is "deceptive" because to the minds of normal people they appear to be something other than what they actually are. The "ultimate" truth of objects is their lack of non-dependence, and is first seen directly in the all-important meditative state known as the "path of seeing." Seeing this truth directly acts immediately to stop the process through which we suffer.

If we do all this we will win a good goal, for we will have found what the verse calls the "*good road*": the path that leads to the land of Enlightenment, the path that never wanders someplace else.

To succeed like this, to actually carry out the path described above—such a good road in the way it combines the open & secret teachings—we will first need to achieve the various conditions that are favorable for us. We'll need to reach the state where our mind is perfectly pliable, and other such qualities. Most of all we will need a *spiritual Guide who can show us this road, and companions in the quest*—genuine friends of a like mind, who are true in keeping each and every one of the Teacher's instructions.

The first thing we are asking our Lama to grant us then is that these true friends *live long and fruitful lives,* that their two legs remain planted here on earth with the immutability of a diamond.

Secondly we are requesting our Lama to *bless and grant us, that* every last bit of *the rain of obstacles* which could ever appear might *stop and end forever.* The first kind of obstacles are those *things outside of us that could stop us now* from reaching our spiritual goals; the main ones would be living in a country where the leaders behave in contradiction to the Dharma—or where they refuse to allow people to enter the Way—by fighting against religion, or the like.

The second type of obstacles are those that are within; examples here would be things like illnesses and harmful spirits that attack your body, or a mental inability to direct your thoughts towards virtuous objects any way you want.

Our Lama noted lastly that for this and the preceding sections there were a good number of essential points covered in traditional advices: what visualizations to perform at each point, how to bring down a flow of nectar to purify oneself, and so on. He said that we should learn these by referring to descriptions found in the more detailed, practical presentations of the Steps of the path.

XIV. A Prayer for Future Care

We have come now to the fourth and final section in the text of the *Source of All My Good*. This is a prayer that, in all our future lives, we may be taken under the care of a Lama, and so gain the strength to reach the end of the various levels and paths. Here again the point is covered in a single verse of the root text:

(14)

In all my lives
May I never live
Apart from my perfect lamas,

May I bask
In the glory
Of the Dharma.

May I fulfill
Perfectly
Every good quality
Of every level and path,

And reach then quickly
The place where I
Become myself
The Keeper of the Diamond.

The verse says, *in all my lives*—that is, in this and in all my future lives to come—*may I never live apart from my lamas,* may I never spend a moment without them. These Lamas are *"perfect"*: they are spiritual Guides who have all the right qualifications; they are the great Lama Lobsang, Lord of the Powerful, who is the Keeper of the Diamond.

And in these lives *may I bask in the glory of the Dharma:* may I seek unceasingly to drink of the Dharma either in the sense of the open and secret teachings, or the teachings that are "deep" and "wide"—the instructions on correct view and living the life of a bodhisattva.

May I then put into actual practice all the Steps of the path, exactly as these Lamas have taught me to do. If I can do so then I will *fulfill* each and *every good quality of the ten levels and* the five *paths*.[100] And I will fulfill them just right, which is to say *perfectly*, or to the highest degree which exists.

---

[100] *Ten levels and five paths:* The ten levels here refer to ten stages at which a bodhisattva attains an exceptional ability to perform the various perfections; they begin with the first direct perception of emptiness.

The five paths represent progressive stages towards the goal of nirvana and omniscience. The first, called the "path of accumulation," begins when a practitioner develops true renunciation for the suffering of life. For a person of the greater way this is accompanied by a full-fledged version of the Wish to gain enlightenment for the sake of others. The second path is called the "path of preparation," and is marked by increasingly refined intellectual understandings of emptiness.

The third path is the "path of seeing," named after the all-important initial direct perception of emptiness. During the subsequent stages of this path one also perceives directly what are called the Four Higher Truths of suffering; the cause of suffering; the end of suffering; and the way to the end of suffering.

The fourth path is the "path of habituation," where one familiarizes themselves repeatedly with the realizations of the previous path, in order to permanently remove all negative emotions and their propensities. This state itself is known as the "path of no more learning," the fifth path. For a practitioner of the lower way this is nirvana, and for one of the greater way it represents the full enlightenment of a Buddha.

The subject of the ten levels and five paths is treated in detail in a standard type of textbook known as the "Presentation of the Levels and Paths." See, for example, the early version by Kedrup Je, entry B9.

And may I reach then the place where I become myself the Lama, Lobsang, Lord of the Powerful Buddhas, *the Keeper of the Diamond.* May I do so *quickly*: in this very life, or at least within seven lifetimes, or no more than sixteen.

Make thus a prayer that you can have the virtuous fortune to make all this come true.

This verse, the one that begins with the words "In all my lives," does not appear at the end of the original text of the *Source of All My Good.* Nonetheless, said our Lama, there is a reason why it is added here in conclusion, and why I have given an explanation of it.[101]

Generally speaking, there are three different objects that you and I can pray for: three goals towards which we can dedicate the power of a great good deed such as the practice we have just completed. The first is to dedicate our virtuous act so that it might turn into a cause for us to achieve Enlightenment. An example of this kind of dedication would be the verse which starts with the line, "By this virtue may all beings..."[102]

---

[101] *Added here in conclusion:* In general the verse is attached to many prayers and rituals as a fitting conclusion. As for dating its first appearance, the verse is not found in the *Mountain* commentary of Tsechokling Yeshe Gyeltsen (1713–1793), nor in that of Akya Yangchen Gaway Lodru (c. 1760), entries B69 and B65, respectively. It does though appear in the explanations of the Second Jamyang Shepa, Konchok Jikme Wangpo (1728–1791), and Keutsang Lobsang Jamyang Monlam (b. 1689). See entries B4 and B3.

[102] *By this virtue may all beings...* These are actually the final lines of Master Nagarjuna's *Sixty Verses of Reasoning,* and are often used nowadays as a prayer of dedication after the good deed of listening to a teaching. The entire verse reads:

> By this virtue may all beings
> Gather the masses of merit and wisdom.
> May they achieve the ultimate two [bodies of a Buddha]
> That the merit and the wisdom produce.

See f. 22b, entry S18, and its commentary by Master Chandrakirti at f. 30a, entry S11.

We can secondly dedicate our good deed to become a cause for the teachings to spread in the world. A typical verse here would be the one that starts with "The prayers of bodhisattva princesses & princes, as many as the drops of water in the Ganges..."[103]

The third way to dedicate a great goodness is so that it brings ourselves and others to be taken under the care of a Lama. Here there are verses like the one with the line about the "matchless Word of the Teacher."[104]

---

[103] *The prayers of bodhisattva princesses & princes:* The original lines are from the third part of a verse description of his spiritual life by Je Tsongkapa entitled *Noble Hopes.* This section is called the "Dedication of All that I Had Done, that the Word Should Flourish in the World," and the entire verse reads as follows:

> The prayers of bodhisattva princesses & princes,
> As many as the drops of water in the Ganges,
> Are all—it is spoken—included within
> A prayer that the Dharma be preserved.
>
> Thus I take the core of virtue
> Created by the good I have done
> And dedicate it to the spread
> Of the Buddha's teaching in the world.
>
> I think of all I've done,
> My hopes in life were noble;
> Oh you have been kind to me,
> Holy Treasure House of knowledge.

See f. 55a, entry B35. The "Treasure House" here, by the way, refers to Gentle Voice—Je Tsongkapa's tutor.

[104] *The teacher unsurpassed:* The lines are often appended to prayers and recitation texts; see for example the version of Je Tsongkapa's *Song of My Spiritual Life* in entry B81, p. 225. The entire verse reads:

> The fact that in my life I've been able
> To meet with the matchless Word of the Teacher
> Is my Lama's kindness, so this good I've done
> I dedicate to the cause that every
> Living being might find themselves
> Under a holy Lama's care.

Once a Lama has taken us into her or his care, the other two goals come then of their own accord. For this reason, any verse dedicated to the third kind of goal is a brief and powerful combination of both dedication & prayer. And this is why the custom prescribed by a great many wise and accomplished saints of our past lineage has been to attach this verse at the end of the work.

❖ ❖ ❖

And so I have finished fully offering up to you all this my explanation of the lines known as *Begging for a Mountain of Blessings*. It is but a brief explanation, barely enough to avoid losing the basic outline.

This *Mountain of Blessings* contains the cream of the holy thoughts of our gentle protector, the great Tsongkapa. It is an extraordinary instruction; it packs a tremendous amount of meaning into but a very few words. In a sense it rips open and lays bare the innermost heart of all the 84,000 great masses of teachings delivered by the Buddhas.

As I mentioned above, the works called *Open Door to the Highest Path* and the *Source of All My Good* were composed by our Lord Lama and delivered as a supplication above the hermitage of the Victor, near the monastery of Radreng, which stands to the north.[105]

Once he had made his supplication, the precious Tsongkapa found himself face to face with each and every Lama of the lineage of the teachings on the Steps of the path to Buddhahood. At the same moment many auspicious signs occurred which portended how the Lord would elucidate these same teachings, making them as clear to us as the Sun in the sky. These and other great deeds would he perform,

---

[105] *The hermitage of the Victor:* The "Victor" here is Dromtun Je, founder of Radreng Monastery—which is located to the north of Lhasa city. See footnote 16 (*The great monastery of Radreng,* page 31) for details.

deeds both powerful and effective in furthering the teachings and the needs of living beings.

Each and every one of us here, those of great intellect and those of lesser, must all emulate the life of the Lord Lama, whose mighty activities spread as far as space itself does. We must do whatever we can to see that these instructions on the Steps of the path to Buddhahood take root and flourish within the minds of ourselves and others.

To accomplish this we must first carry out certain preliminaries: we must collect the power of great good deeds, clean ourselves of our past bad deeds, and make a request to our Lamas for strength. For this we will need a practice, something like the text called the *Preliminary Practices*, or else the *Thousand Angels*.[106]

At the very least we should acquaint ourselves thoroughly with the meaning of the verses of this very brief work. We must make great efforts in a wide variety of related practices, beginning with review meditation to plant desirable seeds in the stream of our mind.

Remember here the words of Tuken Chukyi Nyima:

> What is the Dharma we should learn? And how are we to learn it? There is one and only one being who sees with perfect accuracy each and every crucial point of what we should take up and what we should abandon; this being is the Buddha.
>
> Therefore the Dharma that we choose to learn should be the *Lamp of the Path* by Lord Atisha, and works like the longer and shorter presentations of the Steps which clarify his true intent. The reason is that

---

[106] *The Thousand Angels:* The *Thousand Angels of the Heaven of Bliss* is an extremely important devotional work and meditation centered on Je Tsongkapa. The preliminary practices are a method to prepare oneself properly for a meditation session; a typical version would be that of Pabongka Rinpoche's root Lama, Jampel Hlundrup. See entries B77 and B23, respectively.

these instructions present in their totality the keys which the Buddha himself taught in the open and secret teachings, for actually carrying out the Dharma in one's own life.

It's true that we could choose a different way and devote ourselves in the short term to learning all those weird little scraps of Dharma that somebody supposedly found under the ground, or supposedly fell out of the sky into somebody's lap, or supposedly got handed down by word of mouth from some ancestors of ancient times.

In the long run though all these can only deceive us. This is precisely what happened with great holy beings of the past, authentic masters such as Milarepa and Kyungpo.[107] For a time they deigned to study such works, but later on they were forced to discard them like so much manure, and go on to seek a different Dharma, one that would actually make them enlightened.[108]

---

[107] *Milarepa and Kyungpo:* The great Milarepa (1040–1123) is perhaps the most famed meditator and writer of spiritual poetry in Tibet. In his early years he practiced black magic and used it to harm a great many people. Later he regretted this wrong path and became one of the greatest Buddhist masters of his time, spending a full nine years in intense meditation to achieve the ultimate goal.

The sage Kedrup Kyungpo Neljor (b. 978) was originally a practitioner of the shamanistic Bon religion prevalent in Tibet prior to the arrival of Buddhism. Not reaching the goals he sought, Kedrup Kyungpo travelled to Nepal and India, mastering the Buddhist teachings. He founded numerous monasteries in Tibet and started the Shangpa school of the tradition known as the Kagyu: the Lineage of the Word. For thumbnail biographies see the *Great Dictionary,* entry B80, pp. 2081 and 302, respectively.

[108] *Actually make them enlightened:* See ff. 7a–7b of B60. Tuken Chukyi Nyima (1737–1802) was the third incarnation of the Tuken lineage. His studies were influenced by such eminent Lamas as the Seventh Dalai Lama; the Third Panchen Lama; the great historian and grammarian Sumpa Kenpo Yeshe Peljor; the philosopher Changkya Rolpay Dorje; and most importantly Purbuchok Ngawang Jampa, known for his writings on history and the secret

This too we learn from the lips of Changkya Rolpay Dorje:

> It's true that
> In the past
> Buddhas beyond all counting
>
> Have spoken
> Perfect Dharmas,
> By the millions, in multitudes,
>
> Yet where else
> Is a book
> Like the *Steps to Buddhahood,*
>
> The eloquent
> Instructions
> Of the Lord, Lobsang Drakpa,
>
> Where he
> Takes all
> The highest of words, the teachings
>
> Of Buddhas of Power
> And combines their intent
> Into one, with nothing left out at all.
>
> His is a Dharma
> That benefits all,
> People of high intellect or lesser;
>
> His is a Dharma
> That never errs,
> In its view, meditation, and activities too.

---

teachings. Perhaps the most famous of Tuken's lucid treatises is his *Survey of the Schools of Philosophy.*

Let this then
Be your practice,
Those with the goodness to hear it.[109]

And finally, Gungtang Tenpay Drunme has spoken too:

It may seem
There are many teachings they call "profound,"

But the mind
Settled down in the Dharma sees

That when you go
To take the essence of leisure and fortune,

Your savior will be
The cream of the thought of
    Victors of all three times:

The supreme tradition
Of the Lord, the Victor, Lobsang;

Where every crucial point
Is absolutely complete, and without any error—

The definitions,
And divisions, and order, and all other details

---

[109] *Those with the goodness to hear it:* See f. 2a of his *Door to Freedom*, lines written to himself, at B72. Changkya Rolpay Dorje (1717–1786) was the second incarnation of the Line of the Changkya Lamas, and is said in fact to have been a former life of Pabongka Rinpoche himself. He was Lama to the Emperor of China and instrumental in the publication of the entire Buddhist canon in Mongolian.

Of the path
Where open and secret,
    teaching and practice combine.

For the main stage
Follow review meditation on these,

Every day that goes by
It will plant many seeds in your mind.

Follow as well
For the stages of starting and ending

Just what
Our Lord Lama has taught us to do.[110]

What these Lamas are telling us is that we have at our disposal whatever Dharma we need: we have the longer, and medium, and more brief presentations of the Steps to both the open and secret paths, all set out for us by the Lord, his spiritual Sons, and the various teachers who have followed them.

You have thus in your own two hands a great basket; the lid is wide open, and the basket brims with precious jewels. So don't let your mouth start watering every time you hear somebody spout some meaningless chatter about some new and very oh-so-very "profound" Dharma they've discovered.

---

[110] *Just what our Lord Lama has taught:* The lines are found in a short piece which describes how to meditate on the impermanence of life (see f. 3a, entry B5). Gungtang Tenpay Drunme (1762–1823) spent his early years at the monastery of Labrang Tashi Kyil in east Tibet, and then studied under leading masters of his day at the great Drepung Monastery in Lhasa. He displayed extraordinary talent and received the highest scholastic degree at the age of twenty-two. His collected works span a wide range of subjects including the open and secret teachings of Buddhism, the fine arts, medicine and astrology, and classical grammar.

In Conclusion

Rather take yourself through the great texts and special advices of the wise and accomplished masters of our own tradition, all in the proper order of learning, contemplation, and meditation. Get to a point where you are totally fluent in all the Steps of the path, first by making a conscious effort, and then later in an effortless flow.

Plant and nurture within your own mind, one by one, the various realizations such as disgust with this suffering life, and the Wish to reach enlightenment for every living being, and the ultimate view of reality. Along with these then develop the path of the two secret stages. Work at them until you achieve an extraordinary level of personal experience in each.

Right now you have found a body and life which possess every spiritual leisure and fortune you could ever wish for. This is the only time all this could ever come together for you. Don't let it slip away. Don't waste it on things that are meaningless. Don't waste it on things that have only little meaning. Don't wait until you have lost it forever.

As far as space itself reaches, there live beings who have been your mother. They are old and feeble, they live lives of desperation, and over the reaches of time they have lavished every kindness upon you. For their sake then you must now go and attain this precious gem, the state of secret Union, the being of the One Who Keeps the Diamond.

Make haste, give it all your strength, follow the path given here, reach your goal. You must go now, said our Lama, go, and take the ultimate essence of this one good life you have.

> It is the one immaculate path
> Travelled by each and every Victor;
> It is a treasure of cherished jewels,
> High words from the One of the Sugarcane.[111]

---

[111] *One of the Sugarcane:* An epithet of the historical Buddha, who was born into a group of people called "Those of the Sugarcane."

It is the great book of teachings upon
Profound view and the far-reaching deeds
Come down to us from the royal Regent,
The Invincible Savior, and Gentle Voice.[112]

It descended in a perfect stream
From the Father, Nagarjuna, and his Son;
From Asanga, the Brother, and others too,
Unprecedented from great innovators.[113]
Because of the kindness of one great God,
Along with the Lord named Dromtun Je,[114]
Those of the Land of Snow had the glorious
Fortune to obtain this teaching.

Tibetan translators and Indian masters,
A crowd of wise and accomplished saints,
Undertook thousands of hardships to find

---

[112] *The royal Regent, the Invincible Savior, and Gentle Voice:* The Regent and Savior mentioned here refer to Loving One, Maitreya, the future Buddha who has been placed as regent of the Heaven of Bliss by the present Buddha, Shakyamuni. The lineage of far-reaching deeds motivated by the Wish for enlightenment has come down from Lord Buddha through him, and the lineage of the profound view of emptiness has been passed down to us through Gentle Voice, Manjushri.

[113] *Descended in a perfect stream:* The lines here are describing exactly the same lineages to which Je Tsongkapa made his original supplication when he wrote the text of the *Mountain of Blessings.* The 3rd century Indian masters Nagarjuna and Aryadeva are sometimes referred to as the "Father and Son"—teacher and disciple for the philosophy of emptiness. Master Asanga is also known as the "Brother" since he and the illustrious Vasubandhu had the same mother. Both Nagarjuna and Asanga are spoken of as "innovators" in the sense that they were able to elucidate the scriptures without relying on a previous innovator, and were prophesied as such by the Buddha himself. This subject is treated at length in monastic presentations on the perfection of wisdom such as the *Analysis* of Kedrup Tenpa Dargye, Vol. 1, f. 6a, entry B41.

[114] *The kindness of one great God:* The "God" here refers to Atisha, who with his principal disciple Dromtun Je was chiefly responsible for introducing the teachings on the Steps into Tibet. See also footnote 19 (*Nothing is not a teaching,* page 36).

Millions of scriptures and commentaries
In the Land of the Realized; then here in Tibet
A noble tradition spread and grew,
Till many years later some without wisdom
Began to corrupt it; the sun nearly set.

Then came Tsongkapa, who was in truth
The one called Soft and Glorious Voice.
He opened the way to a new innovation,
The magnificent system of teachings upon
The Steps to the path of all the open
And secret word of the Able Ones.
That day was a powerful blessing bestowed
On the fortunate masses who seek for freedom.

Especially when they call this teaching
The "essence of the highest of words,"
Their praise has a point, for only it fits
The sharpest and middle and dullest of minds.
The Steps are too a spiritual Guide
Who shows the path that is totally pure,
They are eyes that let you see without fail
What things you should practice,
        and what to give up.

This brief abridgement of the keys
Of the deep and widespread Steps of the path
Was drawn from a song of experience
Sung in sixty most glorious tones[115]
By a highly accomplished Saint unmatched
In propounding the open and secret Word:

---

[115] *Sixty most glorious tones:* Refers to 64 different remarkable traits of the speech of the Buddha. The most important of these, as Pabongka Rinpoche himself notes in his *Gift of Liberation,* is the spontaneous ability to speak in a single language, Sanskrit, which is heard by each disciple as their own native tongue. See f. 209b, entry B48.

Pabongka, the Essence of Greatest Bliss,
Lord over all of his secret world.

This excellent explanation then
Is like the mother of the moon,[116]
The treasure trove of a king of kings,
That holds in it all the Buddhas' Word.
By the strength of a trillion Lords of Serpents,
Who uphold the way of the Heaven of Bliss,[117]
May this teaching spread in a glorious spring
Bringing help and happiness far as space.

❖ ❖ ❖

And so ends this very brief explanation of the *Source of All My Good*. It was compiled primarily from a series of notes taken on the 22nd day of the fourth month according to the Mongol system, in the year of the water monkey [1932], at the retreat house known as Tashi Chuling.[118]

The notes are of a teaching delivered by that God of a Secret World, the Protector of All Around Him, the Lord, the Magnificent Keeper of the Diamond: Pabongka, whose kindness knows no equal. At the time he had consented to confer a secret initiation upon a group of some thirty very

---

[116] *The mother of the moon:* The image has a multitude of meanings but, most importantly here, refers to the great outer ocean of Buddhist cosmology. The floor of the ocean was believed in Tibet to be the source of precious jewels. See the *Great Dictionary,* entry B80, p. 2481.

[117] *Way of the Heaven of Bliss:* Refers to the teaching tradition of Je Tsongkapa. The "serpents" mentioned here are the mythical *nagas;* their home was in bodies of water, and it was believed that—so long as they remained in them—the water would never dry up. Here the mighty Lamas of the Lineage are the serpents; because of them, the ocean of enlightenment has come down from Lord Buddha through the teachings like the present book remains.

[118] *The retreat house known as Tashi Chuling:* A hermitage favored by Pabongka Rinpoche and located above an outcropping near Lhasa named "Pabongka Rock." This was the location of Pabongka Monastery, and as a child the Rinpoche was recognized as the reincarnation of this monastery's abbot.

fortunate disciples, including among them the good and glorious Lama of Golok, Jampel Rolpay Lodru, as well as Ganggiu Trulku Rinpoche, the son of Sholkang.[119]

A number of empowerments and instructions upon them were given, centered on the Five Angels of the outer secret world, as well as other aspects of the secret practice of Highest Bliss, according to the tradition of Gantapada. The present explication was granted as the required preliminary to the initiation.

There were also a number of other occasions on which we received brief but very profound instructions on this teaching directly from this very Keeper of the Diamond. For my own benefit, so that I would be able to retain these advices, I had taken down some brief notes and kept several sets of them in my possession. It had always been my intention to organize them into a single work at some later point in time.

The notes came to the attention of the esteemed Yangdzom Tsering, a high lady of noble family. She is one of the great religious sponsors of our land; her faith in the teachings of Lobsang, the King of Buddhas,[120] and in the Lamas and disciples who keep these teachings, is totally unbreakable, unequalled, unshakable as the diamond mountain at the center of the universe.

This noble lady insisted vehemently that I should with all haste come out with a manuscript of the notes which would immediately be carved onto woodblocks and printed. This duty I undertook, not daring to drag my feet or delay the project even so long as it would take to offer the text to others for proofing, editing, and other such tasks.

Along with this encouragement came a second motivation, which was my own desire to benefit fellow

---

[119] *Son of Sholkang:* Sholkang was a powerful government official who assisted the regent of Tibet from the year 1907, and passed away in 1926. See the *Great Dictionary,* entry B80, pp. 3287–3289.

[120] *Lobsang, the King of Buddhas:* Meaning Je Tsongkapa, Lobsang Drakpa.

disciples whose intellect might be as feeble as the one I possess. And so in a great rush I have put together this treatise, combining together all my sets of notes, and the most essential points of whatever I myself was able to grasp with certainty from what he taught.

This labor was accomplished by myself, whose ordination name is Lobsang Dorje, and who hails from the monastery called Den. The writing took place at Ganden Palace, located on the estate of the family of Hlalu. The final pages were completed on the auspicious day of the Meeting of the Angels, during the waning of the moon in the month of *wo*, in the year of the fire monkey [1956].[121]

I pray that this good deed may act as a cause that will give me the strength to further within my own and all other beings' minds the immaculate essence of the open and secret Word: the teachings of the Great Tsongkapa, the Buddha himself returned to us.

She is a sponsor of the Dharma
Whose gifts of faith spread far and wide,
And Yangdzom Tsering in the deed done here
Has given birth to a pure white force.

May this power send her across the spiritual
Levels and paths, with the speed of a carriage,
And bring her quickly to the capital city
Of secret Union, before and beyond all time.

Let goodness grow forever!

---

[121] *The Meeting of the Angels:* A biweekly celebration of the Angel of Diamond. The monastery of Den is located in Kham, east Tibet. The Hlalu were a well-known aristocratic family of old Tibet; their principal holdings were located to the northwest of Lhasa, on the road to Drepung Monastery.

Combined root text of
The Source of All My Good

❦

(1)

The source of all my good
Is my kind Lama, my Lord;

Bless me first to see
That taking myself
To her, or to him,
In the proper way

Is the very root
Of the path, and grant me then
To serve and follow them
With all my strength and reverence.

(2)

Bless me first to realize
That the excellent life
Of leisure I've found
Just this once

Is ever so hard to find
And ever so valuable;

Grant me then
To wish, and never stop to wish,
That I could take
Its essence night and day.

(3,4)

My body and the life in it
Are fleeting as the bubbles
In the sea froth of a wave.

Bless me first thus to recall
The death that will destroy me soon;
And help me find sure knowledge
That after I have died

The things I've done, the white or black,
And what these deeds will bring to me,
Follow always close behind,
As certain as my shadow.

Grant me then
Ever to be careful,
To stop the slightest
Wrongs of many wrongs we do,

And try to carry out instead
Each and every good
Of the many that we may.

(5)

Bless me to perceive
All that's wrong
With the seemingly good things
Of this life.

I can never get enough of them.
They cannot be trusted.
They are the door
To every pain I have.

Grant me then
To strive instead
For the happiness of freedom.

(6)

Grant that these pure thoughts
May lead me to be watchful
And to recall
What I should be doing,

Grant me to give
The greatest care
To make the vows of morality
The essence of my practice;

They are
The root of the Buddha's teaching.

(7)

I have slipped and fallen
Into the sea
Of this suffering life;

Bless me to see
That every living being,
Every one my own mother,
Has fallen in too.

Grant me then
To practice this highest
Wish for enlightenment,

To take on myself
The task of freeing them all.

(8)

Bless me to see clearly
That the Wish itself
Is not enough,

For if I'm not well trained
In the three moralities,
I cannot become a Buddha.

Grant me then
A fierce resolve
To master the vows
For children of the Victors.

(9)

Grant that I may quickly gain
The path where quietude
And insight join together;

One which quiets
My mind from being
Distracted to wrong objects,

The other which analyzes
The perfect meaning
In the correct way.

(10)

Grant that once I've practiced well
The paths shared and become
A vessel that is worthy,

I enter with perfect ease
The Way of the Diamond,

Highest of all ways,
Holiest door to come inside
For the fortunate and the good.

(11)

Bless me to know
With genuine certainty
That when I've entered thus,
The cause that gives me
Both the attainments

Is keeping my pledges
And vows most pure.

Grant me then
To always keep them
Even if it costs my life.

(12)

Bless me next
To realize precisely
The crucial points
Of both the stages,

The essence of
The secret ways.

Grant me then
To practice as
The Holy One has spoken,

Putting all my effort in
And never leaving off
The Practice of the Four Times,
Highest that there is.

(13)

Bless me, grant me that
The spiritual Guide
Who shows me this good road,

And all my true
Companions in this quest
Live long and fruitful lives.

Bless and grant me that
The rain of obstacles,

Things within me
Or outside me
That could stop me now,
Stop and end forever.

(14)

In all my lives
May I never live
Apart from my perfect lamas,

May I bask
In the glory
Of the Dharma.

May I fulfill
Perfectly
Every good quality
Of every level and path,

And reach then quickly
The place where I
Become myself
The Keeper of the Diamond.

Equivalents for Translated Proper Names

෴

As explained in the foreword, selected proper names with symbolic meaning in the original Asian languages have been translated into English. The following list gives the equivalents for these names, in the following order: Romanized Tibetan, phoneticized Tibetan, Romanized Sanskrit, and phoneticized Sanskrit (the latter two only where relevant).

Ancient Ones: Nyingma *(rNying-ma)*

Angel of Liberation: Drolma *(sGrol-ma)*, Tara *(Tara)*

Angel with the Face of a Lion: Sengdongma *(Seng-gdong-ma)*, Sinha Mukhi *(Siṃha Mukhi)*

Ceremony of the Tenth: Tsechu *(Tses-bcu)*

Diamond Queen: Dorje Nelnjorma *(rDo-rje rnal-'byor-ma)*, Vajra Yogini *(Vajra Yogini)*

Frightener: Jikje *('Jigs-byed)*, Bhairava *(Bhairava)*

Gentle Voice: Jampay Yang *('Jam-pa'i dbyangs)* or Jampel Yang *('Jam-dpal dbyangs)*; Manjughosha *(Mañjughoṣa)* or Manjushri *(Mañjuśrī)*

Heaven of Bliss: Ganden *(dGa'-ldan)*, Tushita *(Tuśita)*

Holder of the Diamond: Chakna Dorje *(Phyag-na rdo-rje)*, Vajrapani *(Vajrapāṇi)*

Keeper of the Diamond: Dorje Chang *(rDo-rje 'chang)*, Vajradhara *(Vajradhara)*

Keepers of the Word: Kadampa *(bKa'-gdams-pa)*

Lineage of the Word: Kagyu *(bKa'-brgyud)*

Loving Eyes: Chenresik *(sPyan-ras gzigs)*, Avalokiteshvara *(Avalokiteśvara)*

Loving One: Jampa *(Byams-pa)*, Maitreya *(Maitreya)*

One Who Keeps the Diamond: see Keeper of the Diamond

Practice of Six: Tundruk *(Thun-drug)*

Thousand Angels: Ganden Hlagyama *(dGa'-ldan hla brgya-ma)*

Union of the Spheres: Korlo Dompa *('Khor-lo sdom-pa)*, Chakra Sanvara *(Cakra Saṃvara)*

Virtuous Way: Gelukpa *(dGe-lugs-pa)*

Bibliography

❧

We would like to acknowledge the valuable assistance of Dr. Artemus Engle in compiling the bibliography and notes. Information on many of the works and authors mentioned is as yet far from standardized; dates are taken for the most part from the listings of the U.S. Library of Congress. These are a tremendous resource resulting from the selfless efforts of E. Gene Smith over the entire length of the Library's commendable SFCP foreign texts collection program.

We wish also to thank Dr. C.T. Shen, founder of the Institute for the Advanced Studies of World Religions in Carmel, New York, for kindly facilitating the use of the excellent Tibetan collection at the Institute's Woo Ju Memorial Library. Ven. Ngawang Thupten and Ven. Jampa Lungrik of the Rashi Gempil Ling Kalmyk Mongolian Temple also assisted in researching a number of texts.

Much of the task of compiling this bibliography was undertaken from digital data supplied by the Asian Legacy Library (ALL). We would like to express our gratitude to Sera Mey Tibetan Monastic University and Dr. Robert J. Taylor for their efforts in making this database available to the international scholastic community, without cost.

Some of the works listed below include both Tibetan and Western pagination; these are indicated by "f" (folio) and "p" (page) respectively.

A. Works originally written in Sanskrit

Note: Listed in Sanskrit alphabetical order of author and then title. The word ārya at the beginning of a sutra is not included in its alphabetization. An asterisk (*) after a Sanskrit title indicates that no original version of the title has yet been found, and it has been reconstructed and is still conjectural. An "at" sign (@) indicates that information is not yet established or available.

S1

Atīśa or Dīpaṃkara (Śrī Jñāna) (Tib: Aa-ti-sha or Mar-me mdzad ye-shes), 982–1054AD. *A Light on the Path to Enlightenment (Bodhi Patha Pradīpa)* (Tib: *Byang-chub lam gyi sgron-ma,* Tibetan translation at ACIP TD03947, ff. 238a–241a of Vol. 16 [*Khi*] in the Middle Way School Section [*Madhyāmaka, dBu-ma*] of the *bsTan-'gyur* [*sDe-dge* edition]).

S2

Atīśa or Dīpaṃkara (Śrī Jñāna) (Tib: Aa-ti-sha or Mar-me mdzad ye-shes), 982–1054AD. *A Commentary on Difficult Points in "Light on the Path to Enlightenment" (Bodhi Patha Pradīpa Pañjikā)* (Tib: *Byang-chub lam gyi sgron-ma'i dka'-'grel,* Tibetan translation at ACIP TD03948, ff. 241a–293a of Vol. 16 [*Khi*] in the Middle Way School Section [*Madhyāmaka, dBu-ma*] of the *bsTan-'gyur* [*sDe-dge* edition]).

S3

Avalokitavrata (Tib: (Slob-dpon) sPyan-ras-gzigs brtul-shugs), @. *A Detailed Commentary to the "Lamp of Wisdom" (Prajñā Pradīpa Ṭīkā)* (Tib: *Shes-rab sgron-ma rgya-cher 'grel-pa,* Tibetan translation in three volumes: ACIP TD03849-1, ff. 1a–287a of Vol. 4 [*Wa*]; ACIP TD03849-2, ff. 1b–338a of Vol. 5 [*Zha*]; and ACIP TD03849-3, ff. 1b–341a of Vol. 6 [*Za*] in the Middle Way School Section [*Madhyāmaka, dBu-ma*] of the *bsTan-'gyur* [*sDe-dge* edition]).

S4

Aśvaghoṣa (Tib: (Slob-dpon) rTa-dbyangs), c. 100AD. *The Fifty Verses on Lamas (Guru Pañcā Śikā)* (Tib: *Bla-ma lnga-bcu-pa,* Tibetan translation at ACIP TD03721, ff. 10a–12a of Vol. 78 [*Tsu*] in the Diamond Way Section [*Vajrayana, rGyud*] of the *bsTan-'gyur* [*sDe-dge* edition]).

S5

Asaṅga (Tib: Thogs-med), 350AD. *"The Levels of Listeners,"* a Section from the *"Levels of Deep Practice"* (Yogacaryābhūmau Śrāvakabhūmiḥ) (Tib: *rNal-'byor spyod-pa'i sa las Nyan-thos kyi sa,* Tibetan translation at ACIP TD04036, ff. 1b–195a of Vol. 6 [*Dzi*] in the Mind Only School Section [*Cittamātra, Sems-tzam*] of the *bsTan-'gyur* [*sDe-dge* edition]).

S6

Indrabhūti (Tib: Aindra bh'u-ti), @. *A Ritual for Reaching the Angel Named "The Accomplishment of Wisdom"* (Jñāna Siddhi Nāma Sādhana) (Tib: *Ye-shes grub-pa zhes-bya-ba'i sgrub-pa'i thabs,* Tibetan translation at ACIP TD02219, ff. 36b–60b of Vol. 50 [*Wi*] in the Diamond Way Section [*Vajrayana, rGyud*] of the *bsTan-'gyur* [*sDe-dge* edition]).

S7

Guṇaprabha (Tib: Yon-tan 'od), 650AD. *A Sutra on Vowed Morality (Vinaya Sūtra)* (Tib: *'Dul-ba'i mdo,* Tibetan translation at ACIP TD04117, ff. 1b–100a of Vol. 9 [*Wu*] in the Vowed Morality Section [*Vinaya, 'Dul-ba*] of the *bsTan-'gyur* [*sDe-dge* edition]). A version edited by Rigs-grva Rig-pa'i ral-gri (AKA Blo-bzang 'jigs-med, b. 1763) is reported in the literature.

S8

Candrakīrti (Tib: Zla-ba grags-pa), c. 650AD. *A Detailed Explanation of the 400 Verses Describing the Way of Practice of a Bodhisattva (Bodhisattva Yogācāra Catuḥśataka Ṭīkā)* (Tib: *Byang-chub-sems-dpa'i rnal-'byor spyod-pa bZhi-brgya-pa'i rgya-cher 'grel-pa,* Tibetan translation at ACIP TD03865, ff. 30b–239a of Vol. 8 [*Ya*] in the Middle Way School Section [*Madhyāmaka, dBu-ma*] of the *bsTan-'gyur* [*sDe-dge* edition]).

S9

Candrakīrti (Tib: Zla-ba grags-pa), c. 650AD. *Entering the Middle Way (Madhyāmaka Avatāra)* (Tib: *dBu-ma la 'jug-pa,* Tibetan translation at ACIP TD03861, ff. 201a–219a of Vol. 8 [*Ya*] in the Middle Way School Section [*Madhyāmaka, dBu-ma*] of the *bsTan-'gyur* [*sDe-dge* edition]).

S10

Candrakīrti (Tib: Zla-ba grags-pa), c. 650AD. *A Clarification of the Verses in "Wisdom" (Mūla Madhyāmaka Vṛtti Prasannapada)* (Tib: *dBu-ma rtza-ba'i 'grel-pa tsig gsal-ba zhes-bya-ba,* Tibetan translation at ACIP TD03860, ff. 1b–200a of Vol. 7 ['*A*] in the Middle Way School Section [*Madhyāmaka, dBu-ma*] of the *bsTan-'gyur* [*sDe-dge* edition]).

S11

Candrakīrti (Tib: Zla-ba grags-pa), c. 650AD. *A Commentary to the "Sixty Verses on Reasoning" (Yuktiṣaṣṭhikāvṛtti)* (Tib: *Rigs-pa drug-cu-pa'i 'grel-pa,* Tibetan translation at ACIP TD03864, ff. 1b–30b of Vol. 8 [*Ya*] in the Middle Way School Section [*Madhyāmaka, dBu-ma*] of the *bsTan-'gyur* [*sDe-dge* edition]).

S12

Candrakīrti (Tib: Zla-ba grags-pa), c. 650AD. *A Commentary to the "Seventy Verses on Emptiness" (Śūnyatā Saptativṛti)* (Tib: *sTongnyid bdun-cu-pa'i 'grel-pa,* Tibetan translation at ACIP TD03867, ff. 267a–336b of Vol. 8 [*Ya*] in the Middle Way School Section [*Madhyāmaka, dBu-ma*] of the *bsTan-'gyur* [*sDe-dge* edition]).

S13

Candragomin (Tib: (Slob-dpon) Tzandra-go-mi), c. 10th century. *Letter to a Student (Śiṣyalekha)* (Tib: *Slob-ma la springs-pa'i spring-yig,* Tibetan translation at ACIP TD04183, ff. 46a–53a of Vol. 2 [*Nge*] in the Epistles Section [*Lekha, sPring-yig*] of the *bsTan-'gyur* [*sDe-dge* edition]).

S14

Jñāna Vajra (Tib: Dzny'a-na badzra), @. *Entering into the Activities for Reaching the Angel (Siddhi Caryāvatāra)* (Tib: *sGrub-pa'i spyod-pa la 'jug-pa,* Tibetan translation at ACIP TD01827, ff. 95a–115a of Vol. 35 [*Ci*] in the Diamond Way Section [*Vajrayana, rGyud*] of the *bsTan-'gyur* [*sDe-dge* edition]).

Dīpaṃkara Śrījñāna: see Atīśa or Dīpaṃkara (Śrī Jñāna)

S15

Dharmakīrti (Tib: Chos kyi grags-pa), c. 650AD. *A Detailed Commentary on Accurate Perception (Pramāṇavārtika)* (Tib: *rGyas-pa'i bstan-bcos tsad-ma rnam-'grel,* Tibetan translation at ACIP TD04210, ff. 94a–151a of Vol. 1 [*Ce*] in the Logic & Perceptual Theory Section [*Pramāṇa, Tsad-ma*] of the *bsTan-'gyur* [*sDe-dge* edition]).

S16

Nāgārjuna (Tib: Klu-sgrub), c. 200AD. *The Foundational Verses on the Middle Way Entitled "Wisdom" (Prajñā Nāma Mūla Madhyāmaka Kārikā)* (Tib: *dBu-ma rtza-ba'i tsig-le'ur byas-pa shes-rab,* Tibetan translation at ACIP TDR03824, ff. 1a–19b of Vol 1 [*Tza*] in the Middle Way School Section [*Madhyāmaka, dBu-ma*] of the *bsTan-'gyur* [*sDe-dge* edition]).

S17

Nāgārjuna (Tib: Klu-sgrub), c. 200AD. *Beyond All Fear: A Commentary to the Root Text on Wisdom (Mūla Madhyāmaka*

Vrttyakutobhaya) (Tib: *dBu-ma rtza-ba'i 'grel-pa ga-las 'jigs med*, Tibetan translation at ACIP TD03829, ff. 29b–99a of Vol. 1 [*Tza*] in the Middle Way School Section [*Madhyāmaka, dBu-ma*] of the *bsTan-'gyur* [*sDe-dge* edition]).

S18
Nāgārjuna (Tib: Klu-sgrub), c. 200AD. *Sixty Verses on Reasoning* (in situ: *Yuktiṣaṣṭhakā Kārikā*) (Tib: *Rigs-pa drug-cu-pa'i tsig-le'ur byas-pa*, Tibetan translation at ACIP TD03825, ff. 20b–22b of Vol. 1 [*Tza*] in the Middle Way School Section [*Madhyāmaka, dBu-ma*] of the *bsTan-'gyur* [*sDe-dge* edition]).

S19
Nāgārjuna (Tib: Klu-sgrub), c. 200AD. *A Letter to a Friend (Suhṛllekha)* (Tib: *bShes-pa'i spring-yig*, Tibetan translation at ACIP TD04182, ff. 40b–46b of Vol. 2 [*Nge*] in the Epistles Section [*Lekha, sPring-yig*] of the *bsTan-'gyur* [*sDe-dge* edition]).

S20
Padmasambhāva (Tib: (Slob-dpon) Padma 'byung-gnas), @. *The Five Pledges (Samaya Pañca)* (Tib: *Dam-tsig lnga-pa*, Tibetan translation at ACIP TD01224, ff. 26b–28b of Vol. 8 [*Nya*] in the Diamond Way Section [*Vajrayana, rGyud*] of the *bsTan-'gyur* [*sDe-dge* edition]).

S21
Parahita (Tib: (Slob-dpon) gZhan-la phan-pa), @. *An Explanation of the Seventy Verses on Emptiness (Śūnyatā Saptativivṛti)* (Tib: *sTong-panyid bdun-cu-pa'i rnam-par bshad-pa*, Tibetan translation at ACIP TD03868, ff. 337a–374b of Vol. 8 [*Ya*] in the Middle Way School Section [*Madhyāmaka, dBu-ma*] of the *bsTan-'gyur* [*sDe-dge* edition]).

S22

Bhāvaviveka (Tib: Legs-ldan 'byed), c. 550AD. *The Blaze of Reasoning: A Commentary to "The Heart of the Middle Way" (Madhyāmaka Hṛdaya Vṛtti Tarka Jvālā)* (Tib: *dBu-ma'i snying-po'i 'grel-pa rTog-ge 'bar-ba*, Tibetan translation at ACIP TD03856, ff. 40b–329b of Vol. 3 [*Dza*] in the Middle Way School Section [*Madhyāmaka, dBu-ma*] of the *bsTan-'gyur* [*sDe-dge* edition]).

S23

Maitreya (Tib: Byams-pa), as dictated to Asaṅga (Tib: Thogs-med), c. 350AD. *The Jewel of Realizations, a Book of Advices upon the Perfection of Wisdom (Abhisamayālaṅkāra Nāma Prajñāpāramitopadeśa Śāstra)* (Tib: *Shes-rab kyi pha-rol tu phyin-pa'i man-ngag gi bstan-bcos mNgon-par rtogs-pa'i rgyan*, Tibetan translation at ACIP TD03786, ff. 1b–13a of Vol. 1 [*Ka*] in the Perfection of Wisdom Section [*Prajñā Pāramitā, Shes-phyin*] of the *bsTan-'gyur* [*sDe-dge* edition]).

S24

Maitreya (Tib: Byams-pa), as dictated to Asaṅga (Tib: Thogs-med), c. 350AD. *Distinguishing between the Middle and the Extremes, a Work Set in Verse (Madhyānta Vibhaṃga Kārikā)* (Tib: *dBus dang mtha' rnam-par 'byed-pa'i tsig-le'ur byas-pa*, Tibetan translation at ACIP TD04021, ff. 40a–45a of Vol. 1 [*Phi*] in the Mind Only School Section [*Cittamātra, Sems-tzam*] of the *bsTan-'gyur* [*sDe-dge* edition]).

S25

Maitreya (Tib: Byams-pa), as dictated to Asaṅga (Tib: Thogs-med), c. 350AD. *The Jewel of the Sutras of the Greater Way, Set in Verse (Mahāyāna Sūtrālaṃkāra Nāma Kārikā)* (Tib: *Theg-pa chen-po mdo-sde'i rgyan zhes-bya-ba'i tsig-le'ur-byas-pa*, Tibetan translation at ACIP TD04020, ff. 1b–39a of Vol. 1 [*Phi*] in the Mind Only School Section [*Cittamātra, Sems-tzam*] of the *bsTan-'gyur* [*sDe-dge* edition]).

S26

Vasubandhu (Tib: dByig-gnyen), c. 350AD. *The Treasure House of Higher Knowledge, Set in Verse (Abhidharmakoṣakārikā)* (Tib: *Chos mngon-pa'i mdzod kyi tsig-le'ur byas-pa*, Tibetan translation at ACIP TD04089, ff. 1b–25a of Vol. 2 [*Ku*] in the Higher Knowledge School Section [*Abhidharma, mNgon-pa*] of the *bsTan-'gyur* [*sDe-dge* edition]).

S27

Vibhūticandra (Tib: (Slob-dpon) rNam-grol zla-ba), @. *A String of Light for the Three Kinds of Vows (Trisaṃvara Prabhāmālānāma)* (Tib: *sDom gsum 'od-kyi phreng-ba shes-bya-ba*, Tibetan translation at ACIP TD03727, ff. 54b–56b of Vol. 78 [*Tsu*] in the Diamond Way Section [*Vajrayana, rGyud*] of the *bsTan-'gyur* [*sDe-dge* edition]).

S28

Śākyamuni Buddha (Tib: Sh'akya thub-pa), 500BC. *The Section Called "The House of the Jewel Trees," Part Two (Gaṇḍa Vyūha; no Sanskrit title in situ)* (Tib: *Shin tu rgyas-pa chen-po'i mdo, Sangs-rgyas phal-po che las, sDong-pos brgyan-pa'i le'u* [AKA *gDong-po bkod-pa*], Tibetan translation at ACIP KL00044-6A2, ff. 1b–341a of Vol. 6 [*Cha*] in the Majority Section [*Avataṃsaka, Phel-chen*] of the *bKa'-'gyur* [*lHa-sa* edition]).

S29

Śākyamuni Buddha (Tib: Sh'akya thub-pa), 500BC. *Verses of Drumsong, King of the Serpentines (Nāgārājabherīgāthā)* (Tib: *Klu'i rgyal-po rnga-sgra'i tsigs-su bcad-pa*, Tibetan translation at ACIP KL00325, ff. 314a–320b of Vol. 26 [*La*] in the Collection of Sutras Section [*Sūtra, mDo-mang*] of the *bKa'-'gyur* [*lHa-sa* edition]).

S30

Śākyamuni Buddha (Tib: Sh'akya thub-pa), 500BC. *The Exalted Brief Presentation of the Perfection of Wisdom, Set in Verse (Ārya Prajñā Pāramitā Sañcaya Gāthā)* (Tib: *'Phags-pa Shes-rab kyi pha-rol tu phyin-pa sdud-pa tsigs-su bcad-pa*, Tibetan translation at ACIP KL00013, ff. 189a–215a of Vol. 1 [*Ka*] in the Other Teachings on the Perfection of Wisdom Section [*Citra Prajñā Pāramitā*, Sher-phyin sna-tsogs*] of the *bKa'-'gyur* [*lHa-sa* edition]).

S31

Śākyamuni Buddha (Tib: Sh'akya thub-pa), 500BC. *An Exalted Sutra of the Greater Way Entitled the Cosmic Play (Ārya Lalita Vistara Nāma Mahāyāna Sūtra)* (Tib: *('Phags-pa) rGya-cher rol-pa (zhes-bya-ba theg-pa chen-po'i mdo)*, Tibetan translation at KL00095, ff. 1b–352a in Vol. 2 [*Kha*] in the Collection of Sutras Section [*Sūtra, mDo-mang*] of the *bKa'-'gyur* [*lHa-sa* edition]).

S32

Śākyamuni Buddha (Tib: Sh'akya thub-pa), 500BC. *The Foundation of Vowed Morality (Vinaya Vastu)* (Tib: *'Dul-ba gzhi*, Tibetan translation in four volumes: ACIP KL00001-1, ff. 1a–380a of Vol. 1 [*Ka*]; ACIP KL00001-2, ff. 1a–505a of Vol. 2 [*Kha*]; ACIP KL00001-3, ff. 1a–435a of Vol. 3 [*Ga*]; and ACIP KL00001-4, ff. 1a–436a of Vol. 4 [*Nga*] in the Vowed Morality Section [*Vinaya, 'Dul-ba*] of the *bKa'-'gyur* [*lHa-sa* edition]).

S33

Śākyamuni Buddha (Tib: Sh'akya thub-pa), 500BC. *The Divisions of Vowed Morality (Vinaya Vibhaṃga)* (Tib: *'Dul-ba rnam-par 'byed-pa*, Tibetan translation in four parts: ACIP KL00003-1, ff. 30a–413a of Vol. 5 [*Ca*]; ACIP KL00003-2, ff. 1b–402a of Vol. 6 [*Cha*]; ACIP KL00003-3, ff. 1a–423a of Vol. 7 [*Ja*]; and ACIP KL00003-4, ff. 1a–386a of Vol. 8 [*Nya*] in the Vowed Morality Section [*Vinaya, 'Dul-ba*] of the *bKa'-'gyur* [*lHa-sa* edition]).

S34

Śākyamuni Buddha (Tib: Sh'akya thub-pa), 500BC. *An Exalted Sutra of the Greater Way Requested by the Householder Viradatta (Ārya Vīradatta Gṛhapati Paripṛcchā Nāma Mahāyāna Sūtra)* (Tib: *('Phags-pa) Khyim-bdag dPas-byin gyis zhus-pa zhes-bya-ba theg-pa chen-po'i mdo* (variant spellings *dPa'* and *dPal*), Tibetan translation in ACIP KL00072, ff. 339a–355a of Vol. 5 [*Ca*] in the Pile of Jewels Section [*Ratna Kūṭa, dKon-brtzegs*] of the *bKa'-'gyur* [*lHa-sa* edition]).

S35

Śākyamuni Buddha (Tib: Sh'akya thub-pa), 500BC. *The Great Book of Secrets Entitled "The Perfect Kiss" (Sampuṭi Nāma Mahātantra)* (Tib: *Yang-dag-par sbyor-ba zhes-bya-ba'i rgyud chen-po,* Tibetan translation at ACIP KL00381, ff. 354b–482a of Vol. 3 [*Ga*] in the Diamond Way Section [*Vajrayana, rGyud*] of the *bKa'-'gyur* [*lHa-sa* edition]).

S36

Śāntideva (Tib: Zhi-ba lha), c. 750AD. *A Guide to the Bodhisattva's Way of Life (Bodhisattva Caryāvatāra)* (Tib: *Byang-chub sems-dpa'i spyod-pa la 'jug-pa,* Tibetan translation at ACIP TD03871, ff. 1b–40a of Vol. 10 [*La*] in the Middle Way School Section [*Madhyāmaka, dBu-ma*] of the *bsTan-'gyur* [*sDe-dge* edition]).

S37

Saraha (Tib: (Slob-dpon) Sa-ra-ha), @. *The One Filled with Wisdom: A Commentary on Difficult Points in the Glorious Secret Teaching of the Buddha Skull (Śrī Buddhakapāla Tantra Pañjikā Jñāna Vatī Nāma)* (Tib: *dPal sangs-rgyas thodpa'i rgyud kyi dka'-'grel ye-shes ldan-pa zhes-bya-ba,* Tibetan translation at ACIP TD01652, ff. 104b–150a of Vol. 25 [*Ra*] in the Diamond Way Section [*Vajrayana, rGyud*] of the *bsTan-'gyur* [*sDe-dge* edition]).

S38

@. *The Great Dictionary (Mahāvyutpatti)* (Tib: *Bye-brag tu rtogs-par byed-pa chen-po,* Tibetan translation at ACIP TD04346, ff. 1b–131a of Vol. 1 [*Co*] in the Miscellany Section [*Citra, sNa-tsogs*] of the *bsTan-'gyur* [*sDe-dge* edition]).

B. Works originally written in Tibetan

Note: Listed in Tibetan alphabetical order of author and then title. An "at" sign (@) indicates that information is not yet established or available.

B1
Kirti Blo-bzang 'phrin-las, 1849–1905. *A Brief Word-by-Word Commentary on "Begging for a Mountain of Blessings" (Byin-rlabs spungs-zhus kyi tsig-'grel nyung-bsdus*, ACIP S25195), ff. 1a–4a.

B2
Kirti Blo-bzang 'phrin-las, 1849–1905. *A Brief Commentary on the "Source of All My Good" (Yon-tan gzhir-gyur-ma'i 'grel-pa nyung-bsdus*, ACIP S25196), ff. 1a–7a.

B3
Ke'u-tsang Blo-bzang 'jam-dbyangs smon-lam, b. 1689. *A Recitation to Engage in the Six Preliminary Practices to the Steps to the Path to Enlightenment, Arranged like the Flow of a River (Byangchub lam gyi rim-pa'i sngon-'gro sbyor-ba'i chos drug gi ngag'don chu-'babs su bkod-pa*, ACIP S25214), ff. 1a–105a.

B4
('Jam-dbyangs bzhad-pa sku-phreng gnyis-pa) dKon-mchog 'jigs-med dbang-po, 1728–1791. *How to Engage in the Six Preliminary Practices: Dissection Instructions on the Steps of the Path to Enlightenment Entitled "Word of the Glorious Gentle Voice" (Lam-rim dmar-khrid 'Jamdpal zhal-lung gi sngon-'gro sbyor-ba'i chos-drug nyams-su len-tsul*, ACIP S25209), ff. 1a–3b.

B5
(Gung-thang) dKon-mchog bstan-pa'i sgron-me, 1762–1823. *Versed Advices on How to Meditate on Impermanence (Mirtag-pa sgom-tsul gyi bslab-bya tsigs-su bcad-pa*, ACIP S00945), ff. 1a–3b.

(rGyal mkhansprul) sKal-bzang grags-pa rgya-mtso: see (Gung-thang) Blo-gros rgya-mtso

B6
(T'a-la'i sku-phreng bdun-pa, rGyal-ba) bsKal-bzang rgya-mtso, 1708–1757. *The Song of the Pure One, of Great Meaning: A Separate Collection of Advices, along with Poems and Spiritual Songs, Related to the Practice of Developing the Good Heart (Blo-sbyong dang 'brel-ba'i gdams-pa dang snyan-mgur gyi rim-pa phyogs gcig tu bkod-pa Don-ldan Tsangs-pa'i sgra-dbyangs,* ACIP S05847), ff. 1a–53b.

B7
mKhas-grubs rje (dGe-legs dpal bzang-po), 1385–1438. *Entry Point for the Faithful: The Miraculous and Awe-Inspiring Biography of Our Venerable Lama, the Great Tsongkapa (rJe-btzun bla-ma Tzong-kha-pa chen-po'i ngo-mtsar rmad-du byungba'i rnam-par thar-pa dad-pa'i 'jug-ngogs,* ACIP S05259), ff. 1a–71b.

B8
mKhas-grubs rje (dGe-legs dpal bzang-po), 1385–1438. *A Precious Harvest: A Presentation of the Briefest Part of a Veritable Ocean, the Secret Biography of the Precious Lord, Tsongkapa (rJe rin-po-che'i gsang-ba'i rnam-thar rgya-mtso ltabu las cha-shas nyung-ngu zhig yongs-su brjod-pa'i gtam rin-po-che'i snye-ma,* ACIP S05261), ff. 1a–16b.

B9
mKhas-grubs rje (dGe-legs dpal bzang-po), 1385–1438. *Stealing the Hearts of the Wise: A Presentation of the Levels and Paths (Sa-lam gyi rnam-gzhag mkhas-pa'i yid-'phrog,* ACIP S05495), ff. 1a–12b.

B10
(Co-ne bla-ma) Grags-pa bshad-sgrub, 1675–1748. *The Sun That Illuminates the True Intent of the Entire Mass of Realized Beings, the Victors and All Their Sons and Daughters: A*

Commentary upon the "Treasure House of Higher Knowledge" (*Chos-mngon mdzod kyi t'ikka rGyal-ba sras bcas 'phags-tsogs thams-cad kyi dgongs-don gsal-bar byed-pa'i nyi-ma*, ACIP S00027), ff. 1a–211a.

B11

(rGyal-ba) dGe-'dun grub, 1391–1474. *Illumination of the Path to Freedom: An Explanation of the Holy "Treasure House of Higher Knowledge"* (*Dam-pa'i Chos-mngon-pa'i mdzod kyi rnam-par bshad-pa Thar-lam gsal-byed*, ACIP S05525), ff. 1a–227a.

B12

rGyal mkhan-po (Grags-pa rgyal-mtsan), 1762–1836, ed. *Notes to a Teaching on the "Source of All My Good"* (*Yon-tan gzhir-gyur-ma'i khrid kyi zin-bris*, ACIP S25216), ff. 1a–5b. The person who gave the teachings is identified in the work's colophon at the St. Petersburg Library catalog ref. 02058, and 05645, only as sKyabs-mgon rin-po-che.

B13

('Brom-ston rje) rGyal-ba'i 'byung-gnas, 1005–1064. *A Work Applying the "Tree of Faith," Lines Composed by That King of the Dharma, Dromtun Je, to Inspire Himself to Action* (*'Brom chos kyi rgyal-po nyid kyis mdzad-pa'i Rang-rgyud la bskul-ma 'debs-pa'i Dad-pa'i ljon-shing dang sbyar-ba*, ACIP S25204), ff. 135a–147a.

B14

('Brom-ston rJe) rGyal-ba'i 'byung-gnas, 1005–1064. *"Exhorting Myself to Practice the Dharma with the Magic Tree of Faith," Composed by That King of the Dharma, Dromtun Je* (*'Brom chos kyi rgyal-pos mdzad-pa'i rang-rgyud la skul-ma 'debs pa'i dad-pa'i ljon-shing dang sbyor-ba'i chos*, ACIP S25198), pp. 566–590.

B15

('Brom-ston rJe) rGyal-ba'i 'byung-gnas, 1005–1064. *Selections from Dromtun Je ('Brom-ston-pa'i gsung-btus*, ff. 53a–55a in the section entitled *'Brom gyi gsung*, ff. 45a–55a in *Legs-par bshad-pa bKa'-gdams rin-po-che'i gsung gi gces-btus nor-bu'i bang-mdzod*, ACIP S06971), ff. 1a–297a.

B16

('Brom-ston rJe) rGyal-ba'i 'byung-gnas, 1005–1064. *Dromtun Je's Latter Epistle to Shangtrang Kaberchung ('Brom-ston-pas Zhang-phrang kha-ber chung la springs-yig phyi-ma*, ff. 45a–52b in the section entitled *'Brom gyi gsung*, ff. 45a–55a in *Legs-par bshad-pa bKa'-gdams rin-po-che'i gsung gi gces-btus nor-bu'i bangmdzod*, ACIP S06971), ff. 1a–297a.

B17

rGyal-tsab rje (Dar-ma rin-chen), 1364–1432. *Unerring Illumination of the Path to Freedom: An Explication of "The Commentary on Accurate Perception, Set in Verse" (Tsad-ma rnam-'grel gyi tsig-le'ur byas-pa'i rnam-bshad Thar-lam phyin-ci-ma-log-par gsal-bar byed-pa*, ACIP S05450), ff. 1a–436b, plus one extra folio.

B18

(lCang-skya) Ngag-dbang blo-bzang chos-ldan, 1642–1714. *An Easy Path to Omniscience: Verses of Advice on the Steps of the Path to Enlightenment (Byang-chub lam gyi rim-pa'i gdams-pa'i tsigs su bcad-pa Kun-mkhyen bde-lam*, ACIP S00464), ff. 2a–197a (incomplete).

B19

Ngag-dbang ye-shes thub-bstan rab-'byams-pa, c. 19th century. *Extracting the Essence for Those with the Fortune to Hear: A Detailed Explanation of the Renowned 'Lamp of Blessings'—Instructions in the Form of a Prayer to Achieve the Path of the Open and Secret Teachings, Complete and Without*

Error (mDosngags lam gyi lus yongs-rdzogs tsang la ma-nor-ba smonlam gyi tsul du gdams-pa Byin-rlabs spungs-zhu-mar grags-pa'i rnam-bshad skal-bzang rna-ba'i bcud-len, ACIP S25217), 24 ff.

B20

(T'a-la'i sku-phreng lnga-pa, lNga-pa chen-po, rGyal-ba) lNga-pa chen-po Ngag-dbang blo-bzang rgya-mtso, 1617–1682. *The Lake That Reflects a Million Moons: Steps of Lucid Instruction Related to the Two Systems, for Those of Highest, Lowest, and Middling Capacity (mChog dman bar-pa rnams la lugs-zung dang 'brel-pa'i bslab-bya gsal-bar ston-pa'i rim-pa Zla-ba 'bum-phrag 'char-ba'i rdzing-bu*, ACIP S05666), ff. 1a–40b.

B21

(T'a-la'i sku-phreng lnga-pa, lNga-pa chen-po, rGyal-ba) lNga-pa chen-po Ngag-dbang blo-bzang rgya-mtso, 1617–1682. *The Word of Gentle Voice: A Guide Book for the Steps on the Path to Enlightenment (Byang-chub lam gyi rim-pa'i 'khrid-yig 'Jam-pa'i dbyangs kyi zhal-lung*, ACIP S05637), ff. 1a–95a.

B22

mChims 'Jam-pa'i dbyangs (ᴀᴋᴀ mChims 'Jam-dpal dbyangs), b. 1280. *The Jewel of Higher Knowledge: A Commentary upon the "Treasure House of Higher Knowledge, Set in Verse" (Chos mngon-pa'i mdzod kyi tsig-le'ur byas-pa'i 'grel-pa mNgon-pa'i rgyan*, ACIP S06954), in two volumes: ff. 1a–151b and 296a–430b, respectively. Commonly known as *The Chim Commentary to the Treasure House (mChims mDzod).*

B23

(Dvags-po bla-ma rin-po-che) 'Jam-dpal lhun-grub, @. *Necklace of Good Fortune: The Preliminaries to the Speedy Path— Direct Instructions on the Steps to the Path of Enlightenment, Arranged in Sections for Easy Reading (Byang-chub lam gyi rim-pa'i dmar-khrid myur-lam gyi sngon-'gro'i ngag 'don gyi rim-pa khyer-bde bklag-chog bskal-bzang mgrin-rgyan,* ACIP S25212), pp. 132–159.

B24

('Jam-dbyangs bzhad-pa sku-phreng dang-po) 'Jam-dbyangs bzhad-pa'i rdo-rje, Ngag-dbang brtzon-'grus, 1648–1721. *The String of Jewels That Grant Your Every Wish; a Vast Sea in which You Can Frolic, Swimming in Bliss & Benefit; a Veritable Ocean Spreads Far & Wide, Bringing the Teachings of the Able Buddhas to Every Land; in Brief, the Instructions on How to Depict, in Painted Form, 153 Scenes of the Holy Life of That Illustrious and Holy Being, Je Tsongkapa (rJe-btzun Tzong-kha-pa chen-po'i rnam-thar ras-bris kyi tsul brgya nga-gsum-pa Tzinta ma-ṇi'i phreng-ba Thub-bstan rgyas-byed phan-bde'i rol-mtso chen-po,* ACIP S00072), ff. 1a–26b.

B25

'Jigs-med bsam-gtan, c. 19th century. *White Lotus That Blossoms in the Light of the Moon: A Commentary on the Literal Meaning of the Words of the "Source of All My Good" (Yon-tan gzhir-gyur-ma'i 'grel-pa tsig-don ku-mud bzhad-pa'i zla-'od,* ACIP S25220), @. A work by the same name is said in this source to have been authored by Zhang-ston bsTan-pa rgya-mtso dpal bzang-po (see entry B40). The St. Petersburg Library catalog ref. 02804 also gives the author of a text by this name as Paṇ-rgyan bsTan-pa rgya-mtso.

B26

rJe Tzong-kha-pa (Blo-bzang grags-pa), 1357–1419. *The Great Book on the Steps of the Path, Composed by the Great One, the Incomparable Tsongkapa (mNyam-med Tzong-kha-pa chen-pos mdzad-pa'i Byang-chub lam-rim che-ba,* ACIP S05392), ff. 1a–523a.

B27

rJe Tzong-kha-pa (Blo-bzang grags-pa), 1357–1419. *Letter of Advice to Yunten Gyatso, an Official of Tulung (sTod-lungs-pa Yon-tan rgya-mtso la gdams-pa,* ACIP S05275-100), f. 208a.

B28

rJe Tzong-kha-pa (Blo-bzang grags-pa), 1357–1419. *A Reply in the Way of Instruction on the Summary of the Collection of the Supreme Doctrine of the Conqueror, the Glorious and Excellent Wisdom of the Holder of the Four Scriptures (sDom-brtzon sde-snod 'dzin-pa rGyal-ba'i ringlugs-pa chen-po dKa'-bzhi 'dzin-pa Shes-rab dpal bzangpo'i gsung lan,* ACIP S05275-76b), ff. 173b–176b.

B29

rJe Tzong-kha-pa (Blo-bzang grags-pa), 1357–1419. *The Method of Supplicating the Lineage of the Stages of the Path to Enlightenment: Door to the Highest Path (Door to the Highest Path) (Byang-chub lam gyi rim-pa'i brgyud-pa rnams la gsol-ba 'debs-pa'i rim-pa lam-mchog sgo-'byed (Lam-mchog sgo-'byed),* ACIP S05275-1), ff. 1a–3b. The text of the *Source of All My Good (Yon-tan gzhir-gyur-ma)* is inside this work at ff. 2a–3a.

B30

rJe Tzong-kha-pa (Blo-bzang grags-pa), 1357–1419. *A Brief Presentation of the Practice of the Steps of the Path to Buddhahood, Composed in the Form of Notes (Byang-chub lam gyi rim-pa'i nyams-len gyi rnam-gzhag mdor-bsdus te brjed-byang du byas-pa,* ACIP S05275-59), ff. 55b–58a. Also commonly known as *Songs of My Spiritual Life (rJe Rin-po-che'i nyams-mgur).*

B31

rJe Tzong-kha-pa (Blo-bzang grags-pa), 1357–1419. *The Highway of Bodhisattvas: An Elucidation of Bodhisattva Morality (Byang-chub sems-dpa'i tsul-khrims kyi rnam-bshad byang-chub gzhung-lam,* ACIP S05271), ff. 1a–108b.

B32

rJe Tzong-kha-pa (Blo-bzang grags-pa), 1357–1419. *The Illumination of the True Thought, an Explanation of the Magnificent Classical Commentary Entitled "Entering the Middle Way"* (bsTan-bcos chen-po dBu-ma la 'jug-pa'i rnam-bshad dGongs-pa rab-gsal, ACIP ST05408), ff. 1a–288b.

B33

rJe Tzong-kha-pa (Blo-bzang grags-pa), 1357–1419. *Epistle Dispatched in Response to a Letter from That Immaculate Spiritual Guide, the Great Abbot of Tsako, Ngawang Drakpa, in Which He Informed Je Tsongkapa that He Had Established an Exceptional and Unprecedented Group of Monks in the Eastern Land of Gyalmo Rong* (Yang-dag-pa'i dge-ba'i bshes-gnyen Tsa-kho-ba mkhan-chen Ngag-dbang grags-pas, Shar rgyal-mo rong du sngon med-pa'i rab tu byung-ba'i sde khyad-par-can btzugs nas phrin-yig springs byung-ba'i lan, ACIP S05275-84), ff. 191b–193b.

B34

rJe Tzong-kha-pa (Blo-bzang grags-pa), 1357–1419. *Source of All My Good* (Yon-tan gzhir-gyur-ma), see B79.

B35

rJe Tzong-kha-pa (Blo-bzang grags-pa), 1357–1419. *A Brief Account of My Own Spiritual Life* (Rang-gi rtogs-pa brjod-pa mdo-tzam du bshad-pa (rTogs-brjod 'dun legs-ma), ACIP S05275-58), ff. 52b–55b.

B36

rJe Tzong-kha-pa (Blo-bzang grags-pa), 1357–1419. *The 'Discussion of Disgust with Cyclic Life': Verses to Exhort Myself to Spiritual Practice* (Rang la bskul-ba'i tsigs-su bcad-pa 'khor-ba las skyo-ba'i gtam, ACIP S05275-134), ff. 270b–273a.

B37

rJe Tzong-kha-pa (Blo-bzang grags-pa), 1357–1419. *The Three Principal Paths (Lam gtzo rnam gsum,* ACIP S05275-85), ff. 193b–194b.

B38

rJe Tzong-kha-pa (Blo-bzang grags-pa), 1357–1419. *The Brief Essence of the Ocean of Vowed Morality: A Work Outlining the Vows of Individual Freedom (So-sor thar-pa'i sdom-pa gtan la dbab-pa 'Dul-ba rgya-mtso'i snying-po bsdus-pa,* ACIP S05275-63), ff. 61a–62a.

B39

rJe Tzong-kha-pa (Blo-bzang grags-pa), 1357–1419. *The Golden Harvest of Attainments: An Elucidation of the Morality of the Way of the Secret Word (gSang-sngags kyi tsul-khrims kyi rnam-bshad dNgosgrub kyi snye-ma,* ACIP S05270), ff. 1a–70b.

B40

(Zhang-ston) bsTan-pa rgya-mtso dpal bzang-po, @. *White Lotus That Blossoms in the Light of the Moon: A Commentary on the Literal Meaning of the Words of the "Source of All My Good" (Yontan gzhir-gyur-ma'i 'grel-pa tsig-don ku-mud bzhad-pa'i zla-'od,* ACIP S25211), ff. 1a–7a. A work by the same name is said in this source to have been authored by 'Jigs-med bsam-gtan (see entry B25). The St. Petersburg Library catalog ref. 02804 also gives the author as Paṇ-rgyan bsTan-pa rgya-mtso, and the work as 7 ff. in Vol. 2 [*Kha*] of his collected works.

B41

(mKhas-grub) bsTan-pa dar-rgyas, 1493–1568. *The Garland of White Lotuses: A Fine Explanation of Dialectical Analysis for the Classical Commentary Entitled "The Ornament of Realizations," Along with Its Own Commentary (bsTan-bcos mNgon-par rtogs-pa'i rgyan 'grel-pa dang bcas-pa'i mtha'-dpyod legs-par bshad-pa Pad-ma dkar-po'i 'phreng-ba,* ACIP SE00001) in 8 volumes: Vol. 1, ff. 1a–77a; Vol. 2, ff. 1a–54a; Vol. 3, ff. 1a–56a; Vol. 4, ff.

1a–55a; Vol. 5, ff. 1a–20a; Vol. 6, ff. 1a–68a; Vol. 7, ff. 1a–25a; Vol. 8, ff. 1a–27a.

B42

(mKhas-grub) bsTan-pa dar-rgyas, 1493–1568. *An Illumination of the "Jewel of the Essence of Good Explanation": An Overview of the Root Text and Commentary to the Classical Commentary Known as "The Jewel of Realizations"* (bsTan-bcos mNgon-par rtogs-pa'i rgyan rtza-'grel gyi spyi-don rNam-bshad snying-po rgyan gyi snang-ba phar-phyin spyi-don, ACIP S00009), in 6 volumes: Vol. 1 (commentary to the first chapter), ff. 1a–141a; Vol. 2 (second chapter), ff. 1a–37a; Vol. 3 (third chapter), ff. 1a–15a; Vol. 4 (fourth chapter), ff. 1a–65a; Vol. 5 (fifth through seventh chapters), ff. 1a–21a; and Vol. 6 (eighth chapter), ff. 1a–24a.

B43

(Pha) Dam-pa sangs-rgyas, d. 1117?. *The Hundreds: Advices of the Exalted Dampa Sangye of Dingri* (rJe-btzun dam-pa sangs-rgyas kyi zhal-gdams ding-ri brgya-rtza-ma, ACIP S07006), ff. 1a–11a.

B44

(Khal-kha) Dam-tsig rdo-rje, c. 18th century. *A River of Blessings Arranged in a Stream: Prayers for the Steps of the Path, Along with "Opening the Gate to the Supreme Path: Supplications to the Lineage Lamas of the Steps of the Path"; "Golden Harvest of Attainments: Supplications for the Transmission of Blessings"; "Completing the Two Collections: Supplications for the Seven-step Method for Developing the Good Heart"; Combined with "Spontaneous Present of Each of the Three Bodies: Supplications for the Great Seal"; Incantations to Vanquish Demons; Offering of the Secret World, and Hundred Syllables of the One Gone Thus* (Lam-rim bla-ma brgyudpa'i gsol-'debs lam-mchog sgo-'byed, Byin-rlabs nye-brgyud kyi gsol-'debs dngos-grub snye-ma, Blo-sbyong don-bdunma'i gsol-'debs tsogs-gnyis rab-rdzogs-ma, Phyag-chen gsol'debs lhun-grub sku-gsum-ma rnams la so-sor *kha-skong sbyar-ba dang, bDud tsar-gcod-pa'i sngags dang De-bzhingshegs-pa'i yig-brgya gsung-chos kyi maṇḍal, Lam-rim smonlam bcas phyogs-gcig-tu bsgrigs-pa byin-rlabs chu-rgyun,* ACIP S25218), @ ff.

B45
Don-grub rgyal-mtsan, AKA Ye-shes don-grub bstanpa'i rgyal-mtsan, @, ed. *Collected Treasure of Beloved Jewels: A Fine Explanation of Selected Teachings of the Precious Kadampas (Legs-par bshad-pa bKa'-gdams rinpo-che'i gsung gi gces-btus nor-bu'i bang-mdzod,* ACIP S06971), ff. 1a–297a.

Pha dam-pa sangs-rgyas: see (Pha) Dam-pa sangs-rgyas

B46
Pha-bong kha-pa bDe-chen snying-po, 1878–1941. *Brief Notes Taken on the Occasion of Profound Teachings upon the "Source of All My Good" (Khyabbdag rDo-rje-'chang Pha-bong kha-pa dpal bzang-pos byangchub lam gyi rim-pa'i snying-po bsdus-pa Yon-tan gzhir gyur-ma'i zab-khrid gnang skabs kyi brjed-byang mdor-bsdus-su bkod-pa blang-dor lta-ba'i mig rnam-par 'byed-pa,* ACIP S00069), ff. 1a–27a.

B47
Pha-bong kha-pa bDe-chen snying-po, 1878–1941. *The Key That Opens the Door to the Excellent Path: Notes of an Explanation Granted When the Holder of the Diamond, the Good and Glorious Pabongka, Granted Profound Teachings upon "The Three Principal Paths" (rDo-rje 'chang Pha-bong kha-pa dpal bzang-pos Lam-gtzo'i zab-khrid stzal skabs kyi gsung-bshad zin-bris Lam-bzang sgo-'byed,* ACIP S00034), ff. 1a–41a.

B48
Pha-bong kha-pa bDe-chen snying-po, 1878–1941, oral teachings edited by sKyabs-rje Khri-byang rin-po-che (Blo-bzang ye-shes bstan-'dzin rgya-mtso), 1901–1981. *A Gift of*

Liberation, Thrust into the Palm of Your Hand; the Heart of the Nectar of Holy Advices; the Very Essence of All the Highest of Spoken Words, Representing Profound, Complete, and Unerring Instruction Taken Down as Notes during a Teaching, of the Kind Based on Personal Experience, on the Steps of the Path to Enlightenment, the Heart-Essence of the Incomparable King of the Dharma (rNam-grol lag bcangs su gtod-pa'i man-ngag zab-mo tsang la ma-nor-ba mtsungs-med chos kyi rgyal-po'i thugs-bcud byang-chub lam gyi rim-pa'i nyams-khrid kyi zin-bris gsung-rab kun gyi bcud-bsdus gdams-ngag bdud-rtzi'i snying-po Lam-rim rnam-grol lag-bcangs*, ACIP S00004), ff. 1a–392a.

B49
Pha-bong kha-pa bDe-chen snying-po, 1878–1941. *The Magical Wagon of the Supreme Way: How to Put into Actual Practice the Six Practices as a Preliminary to the Path to Enlightenment* (Byang-chub lam gyi rim-pa'i sngon-'gro sbyor-ba'i chos-drug nyams-su len-tsul theg-mchog 'phrul gyi shing-rta*, ACIP S25199), ff. 1a–45b.

B50
Pha-bong kha-pa bDe-chen snying-po, 1878–1941. *Excellent Path of the Conqueror: Direct Instructions on Practice of the Dharma in the Tradition of the Central Lineage of the "Word of the Glorious Gentle Voice" on the Path to Enlightenment, Arranged for the Purpose of Recitation* (Byang-chub lam gyi rim-pa'i dmar-khrid 'Jam-dpal zhal-lung gi khrid-rgyun rgyas-pa dbus-brgyud lugs kyi sbyor-chos kyi ngag-'don khrigs-chags su bkod-pa rgyal-ba'i lam-bzang*, ACIP S25200), ff. 1a–11b.

B51

Pha-bong kha-pa bDe-chen snying-po, 1878–1941. *A Shower of Excellent Words of the Teacher: An Ornament of Profound Instruction of the Practice of Dharma Worn by the Fortunate* (*sByor-chos skal-bzang mgrin-rgyan gyi zab-khrid man-ngag bla-ma'i zhal-lung dge-legs char-'bebs*, ACIP S25210), ff. 1a–84a.

B52

(Bo-dong Paṇ-chen) Phyogs-las rnam-rgyal, 1375–1450. *Bodong Chokle Namgyel's Collected Works (Bo-dong Phyogs-las rnam-rgyal gyi gsung-'bum,* ACIP VS00001–VS00137), in 137 volumes.

B53

Bu-ston Rin-chen grub, 1290–1364. *The Treasure Chest of Jewels of the Highest of Words—A History of Buddhism Which Illuminates the Teachings of Those Gone to Bliss (bDe-bar gshegs-pa'i bstan-pa'i gsal-byed chos kyi 'byung-gnas gSung-rab rin-po-che'i mdzod,* ACIP S12060), ff. 1a–212a.

(sKyabs-rje Pha-bong-kha-pa rjebtzun) Byams-pa bstan-'dzin 'phrin-las rgya-mtso (dpal bzang-po): see Pha-bong kha-pa bDe-chen snying-po

B54

(Gung-thang) Blo-gros rgya-mtso, 1851–1930, ed. *From the Words of the Lodru Gyatso: A Collection of Scattered Notes Taken on the Occasions of the Granting of Instructions on "The Source of All My Good," Offering of the Wish, Instructions on the 8-Line Practice for Developing a Good Heart, and Oral Transmission of and Teaching on the Middle Way, as Well as Empowerment into the 80 Great Accomplishments, and Others (rJe Blo-gros rgya-mtso'i zhal snga nas, Yon-ton gzhirgyur-ma'i khrid, Sems-bskyed mchod-pa, Blo-sbyong tsig-brgyad-ma'i khrid dang, dBu-ma'i bshad-lung, Grub-chen brgyad-cu'i rjes-gnang sogs stzal skabs kyi so-so'i zin-bris thor-bu phyogs bkod,* ACIP S25221), 12 ff.

B55
(dGe-bshes Gro-lung-pa) Blo-gros 'byung-gnas, c. 1100AD. *An Explanation of the Steps to the Path for Entering into the Precious Teachings of Those Who Have Gone to Bliss (bDe-bar gshegs-pa'i bstan-pa rin-po-che la 'jug-pa'i lam gyi rim-pa rnam-par bshad-pa* [popular title: *The Great Book on the Steps to the Teaching (bsTan-rim chen-mo)*], ACIP S00070), in two etext files of 548 ff. total.

B56
(Paṇ-chen) Blo-bzang chos kyi rgyal-mtsan, 1565–1662. *A Compilation of Scattered Works by the Panchen Lama, the Great All-Knowing One (Paṇ-chen thams-cad mkhyen-pa chen-po'i gsung thor-bu-ba phyogs gcig tu bsdebs-pa rnams,* ACIP S05977), ff. 1a–322a.

B57
(Paṇ-chen) Blo-bzang chos kyi rgyal-mtsan, 1565–1662. *The 'Path of Ease, for Traveling to Omniscience,' a Book on the Steps of the Path to Enlightenment, Written in 'Dissection' Style (Byang-chub lam gyi rim-pa'i dmar-khrid thams-cad mkhyen-par bgrod-pa'i bde-lam (bDelam),* ACIP S05944), ff. 1a–33a.

B58
(Paṇ-chen) Blo-bzang chos kyi rgyal-mtsan, 1565–1662. *A Book of Advices for Keeping Your Morality Pure (Tsul-khrims yang-dag-par srung-ba'i man-ngag,* ACIP S05946), ff. 1a–21a.

B59
(Thu'u-bkwan sku-phreng gsum-pa) (Dharma Badzra) Blo-bzang chos kyi nyi-ma, 1737–1802. *Survey of the Schools of Philosophy (Thu'u-bkvan grub-mtha',* ACIP S25197), ff. 1a–22a.

B60
(Thu'u-bkwan sku-phreng gsum-pa) (Dharma Badzra) Blo-bzang chos kyi nyi-ma, 1737–1802. *The Word of Lobsang: A Clarification of the Preliminary Practices Found in the "Word of the*

Glorious Gentle Voice," on the Steps of the Path to Enlightenment *(Byang-chub lam gyi rim-pa 'Jam-dpal zhal-lung gi sngon-'gro'i chos gsal-bar byed-pa Blo-bzang zhal-lung,* ACIP S25193), ff. 1a–32a.

B61

(Paṇ-chen) Blo-bzang thub-bstan chos-kyi nyi-ma, 1883– 1937. *A Prayer Requesting Blessings: An Expansion of the Renowned Commentary of the Meaning (gSol-'debs byin-rlabs spungs-zhus su grags-pa'i don-'grel mdzad-'phro,* ACIP S25201), ff. 88a–91a.

B62

(rGyal-dbang) Blo-bzang 'phrin-las rnam-rgyal, c. 1840– 1860. *The String of Incredible Jewels, the One Highest Gem That Adorns the Teachings of the Able Buddhas: A Spiritual Biography of Tsongkapa the Great, the King of the Dharma ('Jammgon chos kyi rgyal-po Tzong-kha-pa chen-po'i rnam-thar thub-bstan mdzes-pa'i rgyan-gcig ngo-mtsar nor-bu'i 'phrengba,* ACIP SL00191), pp. 1–635 (incomplete).

B63

(Gu-shri bKa'-bcu-pa Mer-gen mkhan-po) Blo-bzang tse-'phel, b. ~1760. *Explaining the Direct Path to Omniscience: Joining the Two of the Precious Words of the Victor and Opening the Door to the Supreme Path (rGyal-ba'i gsung-rab rin-po-che dang lam-mchog sgo-'byed gnyis sbyar te bshad-pa kun-mkhyen nye-lam,* ACIP S25215), ff. 16.

B64

(Gu-shri bKa'-bcu-pa Mer-gen mkhan-po) Blo-bzang tse-'phel, b. ~1760. *Explaining the Excellent Practices of the Conqueror: Joining the Two of the Precious Words of the Victor and Opening the Door to the Supreme Path (rGyal-ba'i gsung-rab rin-po-che dang lam-mchog sgo-'byed gnyis sbyar te bshad-pa rgyal-ba'i lam-bzang,* ACIP S25208), ff. 1a–159a.

B65
(Aa-kya Yongs-'dzin) dByangs-can dga'-ba'i blo-gros, 1740–
1827. *Door for the Fortunate: Engaging in the Six Practices as
a Preliminary to the Steps to the Path to Enlightenment (Byang-
chub lam-gyi rim-pa'i sngon-'gro sbyor-ba'i chos drug skal-ldan
'jug-ngogs*, ACIP S25207), ff. 1a–16a.

'Brom-ston rje: see ('Brom-ston-rje) rGyal-ba'i 'byunggnas

B66
(rJe Kar-ma-pa) Mi-bskyod rdo-rje, 1507–1554. *In Praise of
the Victorious One, the Great Tsongkapa, Written by Je Karmapa,
Mikyu Dorje (rJe Kar-ma-pa Mibskyod rdo-rjes rGyal-ba Tzong-
kha-pa chen-po la bstod-pa mdzad-pa*, ACIP S25219), ff. 4b–5a.

Tse-mchog-gling Ye-shes rgyal-mtsan: see (Tse-mchog-gling)
Yongs-'dzin Ye-shes rgyal-mtsan

B67
('Bras Tre-bo dGe-bshes, 'Bras-spungs mtsan-zhabs) Tse-
dbang bsam-grub, b. 1835. *String of Shining Jewels: An
Explanation of the Rules Contained in the Three Types of Vows —
Those of Individual Freedom, Those of the Bodhisattva, and Those
of the Secret Word (So-thar byang-sems gsang-sngags gsum gyi
sdom-pa'i bslab-bya nor-bu'i 'od-'phreng*, ACIP S00201), ff.
1a–37a (incomplete).

B68
(Tse-mchog gling) Yongs-'dzin Ye-shes rgyal-mtsan, 1713–
1793. *Entering the Door of the Supreme Path: A Series of Prayers
to the Lineage Lamas (Bla-brgyud gsol-'debs kyi rim-pa lam-mchog
sgo-'byed*, ACIP S06129), ff. 1a–40a.

B69

(Tse-mchog gling) Yongs-'dzin Ye-shes rgyal-mtsan, 1713–1793. *The Source of All Attainments: Pith Instructions Clearly Revealing the Meaning of Requesting Heaps of Blessings on How to Develop the Aspiration to Reach the Complete Perfection of the Path (Lam gyi lus yongs-su-rdzogs-pa la smon-lam du bya-ba'i tsul byin-brlab spungs-zhus kyi don gsal-bar stonpa'i man-ngag dngos-grub kun-'byung*, ACIP S06047), ff. 1a–8a.

B70

(Tse-mchog gling) Yongs-'dzin Ye-shes rgyal-mtsan, 1713–1793. *The Ornament of Understanding of the Intelligent: How to Engage in the Six Practices as a Preliminary to the Steps of the Path (Lam-rim sngon-'gro sbyor-ba'i chos drug bya-tsul Blo-bzang dgongs-rgyan*, ACIP S05999), ff. 1a–14a.

B71

(Zhva-lu ri-zur) Rin-chen blo-bzang mkhyen-rab, c. 19th century. *An Easy Road for the Virtuous to Travel to the Heaven of the Sky: Instructions for Undertaking the Deep Practice of the Two Stages of the Secret Teachings of the Holy Queen of the Heaven of Naropa (Vajra Yogini) (rJe-btzun N'a-ro mkha'-spyod-ma'i rim gnyis kyi rnal'byor skyong-ba'i skal-bzang mkha'-spyod bgrod-pa'i bdelam*, ACIP S00064), ff. 1a–96a.

B72

(lCang-skya) Rol-pa'i rdo-rje, 1717–1786. *The Door to Freedom: A Spiritual Song That Exhorts Us to Practice the Teachings (Chos la bskul-ba'i glu-dbyangs Thar-pa'i sgo-'byed*, ACIP S25194), ff. 1a–3b.

B73

(Klu-'bum) Shes-rab rgya-mtso, ᴀᴋᴀ (rDo-sbis dgebshes) Shes-rab rgya-mtso, ᴀᴋᴀ ('Bras klu-'bum rdo-sbi lHa-ram-pa) Shes-rab rgya-mtso, 1884–1968. *A Cloud of Offerings to Please Our Gentle Protector, Our Lama: An Abbreviated Commentary on the "Source of All My Good" (Yon-tan gzhirgyur-ma'i bsdus-'grel 'Jam-mgon bla-ma dgyes-pa'i mchodsprin,* ACIP S25202), ff. 1a–54a.

B74

(Aa-khu-ching Drung-chen) Shes-rab rgya-mtso, b. 1803. *Medicinal Sprouts to Dispel Longing: Notes on the "Source of All My Good" (Yon-tan gzhir-gyur-ma'i zin-bris gdung-sel sman gyi myugu,* ACIP S25203), ff. 1a–14a.

B75

(Stag-tsang Lo-tz'a-ba) Shes-rab rin-chen, b. 1405. *An Elaborate Lotus of Faith: A Day of Singing Words of Praise, a Brief Expression of the Nature of the Glorious Lobsang Drakpa, Great Holder of the Teachings beyond Equal, Here in the Land of Snowy Mountains (Gangs ri'i khrod 'dir spyi'i bstan 'dzin chen-po 'gran zla kun bral blo-bsang grags-pa'i dpal gyi ngang tsul mdo tzam du brjod-pa Dadpa'i padma rgyas-par byed-pa'i bstod-tsig gi nyi-ma,* ACIP S25205), ff. 1a–3b.

B76

Sh'a sa na d'i paṃ, @. *Unlocking the Door to the Supreme Path: How to Rely on a Spiritual Friend Is the Root of the Path, in Brief (Lam gyi rtza-ba bshes-gnyen bsten-tsul mdor-bsdus lam-mchog sgo-'byed,* ACIP S25206), ff. 1a–13a.

B77

(rGyud-chen) Sangs-rgyas rgya-mtso, comp. *Thousand Angels of the Heaven of Bliss (dGa'-ldan lha-brgya-ma,* ACIP S06220), ff. 1a–5a (incomplete).

B78

(Paṇ-chen) bSod-nams grags-pa, 1478–1554. *A Lovely Jewel to Adorn the Mind: A Spiritual History of Both the Newer and Older Schools of the Kadampa, the Keepers of the Word (bKa'-gdams gsar-rnying gi chos-'byung Yid kyi mdzes-rgyan,* ACIP S12403), ff. 1a–162a.

B79
sNa-tsogs (Various authors), modern. *A Catalog of Some of the Great Books of Tibet (Bod kyi bstan-bcos khag-cig gi mtsan-byang,* ACIP R00004), 687 pp.

B80
sNa-tsogs (Various authors), modern. *The Great Dictionary of the Tibetan and Chinese Languages (Bod-rgya tsig-mdzod chen-mo)* (Beijing: Mi-rigs dpe-skrun khang, 1985), ACIP R00002), 3294 pp.

B81
@. *A Compendium of Liturgical Texts Which Are Unique to That Isle of the Greater Way, Sera Monastery (Se-ra theg-chen gling gi thun-mong ma-yin-pa'i chos-spyod,* ACIP S25213), 462 pp.

C. Works originally written in English

E1

Chandra, Lokesh. *Tibetan-Sanskrit Dictionary* (Reprint Kyoto: Rinsen Book Co, 1982), 2560 pp.

E2

Das, Sarat Chandra, ed. *A Tibetan-English Dictionary* (Reprint New Delhi: Motilal Banarsidass, 1970), 1353 pp. Also available on microfiche from IASWR.

E3

Edgerton, Franklin, ed. *Buddhist Hybrid Sanskrit Grammar and Dictionary, Volume II: Dictionary* (Reprint New Delhi: Motilal Banarsidass, 1972), 627 pp.

E4

Monier-Williams, Sir Monier. *A Sanskrit-English Dictionary* (Reprint Delhi: Motilal Banarsidass, 1976), 1333 pp. Also available on microfiche from IASWR.

E5

Pabongka Rinpoche. *Liberation in Our Hands*, tr. Khen Rinpoche Geshe Lobsang Tharchin with Artemus Engle (Howell: Mahayana Sutra and Tantra Press), Parts One (1988) and Two (1994).

E6

Roach, Geshe Michael. *King of the Dharma: The Illustrated Life of Je Tsongkapa, Teacher of the First Dalai Lama* (Wayne, NJ: Diamond Cutter Press, 2008), 465 pp.

E7

Roerich, George N., tr. *The Blue Annals [of 'Gos lo-tsva-ba gZhon-nu dpal, 1392–1481]* (Reprint New Delhi: Motilal Banarsidass, 1979), 1275 pp.

E8
Tharchin, Geshe Lobsang, and Artemus B. Engle, tr.
*Nāgārjuna's Letter: Nāgārjuna's "Letter to a Friend" with
a Commentary by the Venerable Rendawa, Zhön-nu Lo-drö*
(Dharamsala, India: Library of Tibetan Works and Archives,
1979), 163 pp.

E9
(Je) Tsongkapa, with commentary by Pabongka Rinpoche.
The Principal Teachings of Buddhism, tr. Khen Rinpoche Geshe
Lobsang Tharchin with Michael Roach (Howell: Classics of
Middle Asia Series, Mahayana Sutra and Tantra Press, 1988),
209 pp.

E10
Vostrikov, A.I.   *Tibetan Historical Literature,* tr. H. C.
Gupta (Calcutta: Indian Studies, Past & Present, 1970),
275 pp., ACIP.

E11
Whitney, William Dwight. *The Roots, Verb-Forms, and Primary
Derivatives of the Sanskrit Language* (Reprint New Haven:
American Oriental Society, 1945), 250 pp., ACIP ref. R00013.

The Diamond Cutter Classics Series

The book you are reading is one of over 100 volumes in the Diamond Cutter Classics Series. For those who are interested in furthering their study of the great ideas of ancient Asia, we provide the following list of titles in the series. They cover original translations of the ancient classics; courses for modern life based upon them; and popular titles conveying the same information to a more general audience.

The titles in Group 5 marked with an asterisk (*) are completed and published, as of June 2023; printed and ebook versions are available from online booksellers worldwide, such as Amazon, as well as from the Diamond Cutter Press at *DiamondCutterPress.com*.

For more information, to follow the translation of these great books live, or to make any inquiry about our work, please visit the Diamond Cutter Classics Series website at *DiamondCutterClassics.com*. We would love to hear from you.

List of Titles

Group 1
Worldview Books for the Modern World

1) The Diamond Cutter:
*   The Buddha on Managing Your Business and Your Life*

2) The Garden: A Parable

3) How Yoga Works

4) The Karma of Love:
*   100 Answers for Your Relationship*

5) Karmic Management:
*   What Goes Around Comes Around,*
*   in Your Business and Your Life*

6) The Tibetan Book of Yoga:
*   Ancient Buddhist Teachings*
*   on the Philosophy & Practice of Yoga*

7) To the Inner Kingdom
*   Quiet Retreat Teachings Series, Book 1*

8) The Magic of Empty Teachers
*   Quiet Retreat Teachings Series, Book 2*

9) Second Sight
*   Quiet Retreat Teachings Series, Book 3*

10) Ripples of Light
*   Quiet Retreat Teachings Series, Book 4*

11) The Essential Yoga Sutra

12) King of the Dharma: The Illustrated Life of Je Tsongkapa

Group 2
Books of the 12 Levels
of the Diamond Cutter Institute (DCI)

24) DCI Book 7:
   Reaching the Diamond World:
   Learning to Touch the Source of All Success

25) DCI Book 8:
   Automatic Leadership

26) DCI Book 9:
   True Innovators:
   The Deeper Causes of Creativity

27) DCI Book 10:
   Impossible Anger:
   Never Get Upset Again

28) DCI Book 11:
   Time Management:
   Using the Inner Conversation

29) DCI Book 12:
   The Art of Gratitude

120) DCI Book 13:
   Problem-Solving Masterpieces

121) DCI Book 14:
   Techniques for Moving Dreams into Reality

Group 3
Foundation Books of the Asian Classics Institute (ACI)
(all translated compilations from ancient classics)

30) ACI Book 1: *The Principal Teachings of Buddhism*

31) ACI Book 2: *Buddhist Refuge*

32) ACI Book 3: *Applied Meditation*

33) ACI Book 4: *The Proof of Future Lives*

34) ACI Book 5: *How Karma Works*

35) ACI Book 6: *The Diamond-Cutter Sutra*

36) ACI Book 7: *The Vows of the Bodhisattva*

37) ACI Book 8: *Death and the Realms of Existence*

38) ACI Book 9: *The Ethical Life*

39) ACI Book 10: *Guide to the Bodhisattva's Way of Life, Part I*

40) ACI Book 11: *Guide to the Bodhisattva's Way of Life, Part II*

41) ACI Book 12: *Guide to the Bodhisattva's Way of Life, Part III*

42) ACI Book 13: *The Art of Reasoning*

43) ACI Book 14: *Lojong, Developing the Good Heart*

44) ACI Book 15: *What the Buddha Really Meant*

45) ACI Book 16: *The Great Ideas of Buddhism, Part One
A Review of ACI Courses 1–5*

46) ACI Book 17: *The Great Ideas of Buddhism, Part Two
A Review of ACI Courses 6–10*

47) ACI Book 18: *The Great Ideas of Buddhism, Part Three
A Review of ACI Courses 11–15*

Group 4
Advanced Books of the Asian Classics Institute
(all translated compilations from ancient classics)

48) ACI Book 19: *The Path to Bliss, Part One*

49) ACI Book 20: *The Path to Bliss, Part Two*

50) ACI Book 21: *The Path to Bliss, Part Three*

51) ACI Book 22: *A Rite of Empowerment into the Secret Teachings of the Lord of Terror (Yamantaka)*

52) ACI Book 23: *The Commitments of the Secret Word*

53) ACI Book 24: *An Overview of the Tantric Path*

54) ACI Book 25: *The Blessing of the Diamond Angel (Vajra Yogini)*

55) ACI Book 26: *Sadhana: Reaching the Angel*

56) ACI Book 27: *The Yoga of the Lama, Part 1*

57) ACI Book 28: *The Yoga of the Lama, Part 2*

58) ACI Book 29: *The Yoga of the Mantra*

59) ACI Book 30: *Lerung: The Art of Tantric Retreat*

60) ACI Book 31: *A Bridge to the Stage of Completion*

61) ACI Book 32: *The Six Yogas of Naropa, Part 1*

62) ACI Book 33: *The Six Yogas of Naropa, Part 2*

63) ACI Book 34: *Continuing with the Stage of Completion*

64) ACI Book 35: *Practice with a Spiritual Partner*

65) ACI Book 36: *The Offering to Lamas*

66) ACI Book 37: *The Complete Practices of the Medicine Buddha*

Group 5
Translations of Ancient Asian Classics

67) *The Principal Teachings of Buddhism*
by Je Tsongkapa (1357–1419),
including a commentary
by Pabongka Rinpoche (1878–1941)

68) *Door to the Diamond Way**
by Je Tsongkapa (1357–1419),
including a commentary by Pabongka Rinpoche
(1878–1941)

69) *Poems from the Tantric College*
by Lobsang Chukyi Gyeltsen,
His Holiness the First Panchen Lama (1565–1662)

70) *Three Treasures: A Buddhist Prayer Book*
    by Dakpo Lama Jampel Hlundrup Gyatso
    (1845–1919), Je Tsongkapa (1357–1419), Gyuchen
    Sangye Gyatso (b. 1550), and His Holiness the First
    Panchen Lama (1565–1662)

71) *Sky Flowers & Magic Shows: The Interaction of Reality*
    by Master Yuance of the Tang Dynasty (613–
    696AD), Book 1 of the Xuanzang's Legacy Series

72) *Neither One nor Many: The Nature & Function of*
    Ultimate Reality by Master Yuance of the Tang
    Dynasty (613–696AD), Book 2 of the Xuanzang's
    Legacy Series

73) *Sunlight on the Path to Freedom:*
    A Commentary to the Diamond Cutter Sutra*
    by Choney Lama Drakpa Shedrup (1675–1748)

74) *The String of Precious Jewels: A Brief Word-by-Word*
    Commentary on Je Tsongkapa's "Essence of the Ocean
    of Discipline"
    by Je Tsongkapa (1357–1419), including a
    commentary by Gyal Kenpo Drakpa
    Gyeltsen (1762–1837)

75) *The Sun which Illuminates the True Thought*
    of All the Able Ones and their Children:
    A Commentary to the "Treasure House of Higher
    Knowledge"
    by Master Vasubandhu (350AD),
    with a commentary by Choney Lama Drakpa
    Shedrup (1675–1748)

76) *All Paths Are One: The Role of Understanding in*
    Achieving Goals
    by Master Yuance of the Tang Dynasty (613–
    696AD), Book 3 of the Xuanzang's Legacy Series

77) *A Door to Emptiness: The Crucial Teaching for*
    Touching the Diamond World*
    by Ngawang Tashi, of the Clan of Sey (1678–1738)

86) *Emptiness Meditations:*
  Learning How to See
  *That Nothing Is Itself**
  by Choney Lama, Drakpa Shedrup (1675–1748),
  with additional instruction from:
  Arya Nagarjuna (200AD)
  Master Kamalashila (775AD)
  Pabongka Rinpoche (1878–1941)
  Trijang Rinpoche (1901–1981)

87) *A Commentary to Nagarjuna's "Sixty Verses*
  on Reasoning"
  by Master Nagarjuna (200AD), with a commentary
  by Gyaltsab Je, Darma Rinchen (1364–1432)

88) *Using Contemplation to Understand How*
  the World Really Works
  by Master Yuance of the Tang Dynasty (613–
  696AD), Book 6 of the Xuanzang's Legacy Series

89) *Great Ideas of the East: A Survey of 101 Enlightening*
  Belief Systems from Ancient Asia
  by Choney Lama Drakpa Shedrup (1675–1748)

90) *Preparing for the Diamond Way: The Mountain*
  of Blessings
  by Je Tsongkapa (1357–1419),
  with a commentary by
  Pabongka Rinpoche (1878–1941)

91) *The Three Turnings of the Wheel: The Interpretation of*
  Historical Periods
  by Master Yuance of the Tang Dynasty (613–
  696AD), Book 7 of the Xuanzang's Legacy Series

92) *Sunlight on Suchness: The Meaning of the Heart Sutra**
  by Choney Lama Drakpa Shedrup (1675–1748)

93) *All the Kinds of Karma**
     by Lord Buddha (500BC)

94) *Deathless Nectar for Helping Others:*
     A Commentary to the "Crown of Knives"
     by Dharma Rakshita (c. 1000AD) & Tenpa Rabgye,
     Throneholder of Radreng (1759–1816)

95) *The Hidden Workings of the World*
     by Master Yuance of the Tang Dynasty (613–
     696AD), Book 8 of the Xuanzang's Legacy Series

96) *Destroying the Darkness in Our Minds: An Explanation*
     of the Seven Books of Reasoning
     by Kedrup Je Gelek Pel Sangpo (1385–1438)

97) *Opening the Eyes of the Fortunate: An Interlude*
     on Emptiness
     by Kedrup Je Gelek Pel Sangpo (1385–1438)

98) *A Gift of Liberation, Thrust into Our Hands*
     by Pabongka Rinpoche (1878–1941)

99) *An Overview of the Middle Way*
     by Kedrup Tenpa Dargye (1493–1568)

100) *An Analysis of the Perfection of Wisdom*
     by Kedrup Tenpa Dargye (1493–1568)

101) *The Illumination of the True Thought*
     by Je Tsongkapa (1357–1419)

102) *A Guide to the Bodhisattva's Way of Life*
     by Master Shantideva (700AD)

103) *The Great Commentary to the Diamond Cutter Sutra**
     by Master Kamalashila (750AD)

104) *A Ship on the Sea of Emptiness: The Wisdom*
     of Nagarjuna
     by Choney Lama Drakpa Shedrup (1675–1748)

Constantly check
Your thoughts, words, and deeds
To stop any wrong to come.

Recollect yourself,
Take the greatest care,
Have a sense of shame,
And consideration;

Use them on
The horse of the senses
When it mistakes the way.

Use your strength
To rein the horse in,
For this is the state of mind

That you can bring
To focus and stay
On any virtuous object

Solidly,
Whatever you want,
However you wish it to be;

And this is why
They sing the praises
Of morality as the way

To reach one-pointedness of mind. [72]

---

[72] *They sing the praises of morality:* The circumstances of the composition of these lines in praise of morality were especially joyful. Je Tsongkapa had ¹ᵗ one of his favorite disciples, Tsako Ngawang Drakpa, to eastern Tibet in ᵒ teach and establish new monasteries. Upon the ordination of the first ʰᵉ area of Gyalmo Rong, the disciple wrote a letter to the Master ᵒᶠ the event. These words are from an exquisite epistle which reply. See f. 191b of entry B33.

Steps Shared with Those of Medium Capacity

Nowhere does it say
Anything else but this:
If you hope to develop

Insight, the training
Of wisdom well,
You must find quietude,
That of concentration.

It says as well
That if you wish to develop
Pure single-pointed mind,

You must have the training
Of morality;
And this is fine advice.

Some brave souls
Claim they'll keep
A lot of different vows,

But it's oh so common
To see them smash
Whatever pledges they've made.

The way of the holy
Is to strive
To maintain their morality pure,

Exactly as
They have agreed
To do so.

Once you see
The truth in this,
Then use your watchfulness,